MORE

GET MORE OUT OF LIFE
WITH LESS COMPLICATION

*Merle –
May you be blessed
with MORE!
with gratitude –
Elise Scheck Bonwitt*

ELISE SCHECK BONWITT
FOREWORD BY SHERYL SANDBERG

First published by Ultimate World Publishing 2020
Copyright © 2020 Elise Scheck Bonwitt

ISBN

Paperback: 978-1-922497-46-8
Ebook: 978-1-922497-47-5

Cover design: Ultimate World Publishing
Layout and typesetting: Ultimate World Publishing
Editor: Marinda Wilkinson
Photograph: Amy Gelb
Cover copyrights: Jim Bosiak-Shutterstock.com

Ultimate World Publishing
Diamond Creek,
Victoria Australia 3089
www.writeabook.com.au

Testimonials

Happiness is a choice . . . the perfect message at the perfect time. Bravo!
Susan Ford Collins, Creator of The Technology of Success and Author of *The Joy of Success*

We all want to know how to get more out of life. Elise shares her wisdom and gives the reader simple tools to discover how to live a happier life with more positivity, gratitude, generosity, balance, connection, serenity, and success.
Amy Gelb, Artist, Photographer and Author of *As Is: Women Exposed*

More is a straightforward and easy guide to change any aspect of your life. Whether you desire more calm, happiness, balance, success, or gratitude, Elise has compiled ideas and practical steps to help you move forward, prioritize your goals, and change your perspective. Her focus on giving more is particularly relevant and inspiring.
Verne Harnish, Founder Entrepreneurs' Organization (EO) and Author of *Scaling Up*

More inspires us to be more positive and take an active role in crafting a happier life for ourselves. Full of inspiring quotes and actionable steps, it is a great handbook for a more fulfilling life.

Jeannette Kaplan, Author, TV personality and Editor of Hispana Global (hispanaglobal.com)

Elise Scheck Bonwitt has found a way to help us quiet the buzzing, future-focused voices in our heads and instead pay closer attention to our blessings in the moment. Her book is an invaluable guide to positivity, persistence, priorities, and some key lessons she's learned which can help reduce our self-criticism, reorient our perspectives, and boost a sense of contentedness. I intend to make this my go-to gift for my closest friends.

Abigail Pogrebin, Journalist and Author

This book is a physical manifestation of my friend, Elise Scheck Bonwitt. She is smart, consistent, studied, practical, and joyous. So grateful I get to benefit from a person who finds ways to give even MORE of herself to me each day.

Kerry-Ann Royes, MBA, President & CEO YWCA South Florida

Elise delivers a personal, practical how-to with simple, meaningful tips to get you out of your own way and on the road to more happiness.

Rochelle Weinstein, USA Today Bestselling Author

Dedication

To my parents, Raquel and Michael Scheck, for being incredible role models and teaching me that I could always be more,

To my husband, Gil Bonwitt, for giving me more love, respect, and support than a young woman could ever have dreamed of, and

To my children, Joshua, Keith, David, Gabriella, and Jessica Bonwitt, for giving me more pride and inspiration than any mom could ask for.

Foreword

If we're lucky, we find true friends in this world.

If we're even luckier, we find them when we're young.

Elise and I met at the start of tenth grade at North Miami Beach High School. She and I became instant friends, and soon there were seven of us: Mindy, Eve, Jami, Pam, Beth, Elise, and me. We called ourselves "the Girls" and still do to this day, even though we are now in our fifties. We've been there for each other through everything— college, dating, marriage, children, loss, work—and lately, COVID-19. We've celebrated joyful milestones together, picked one another up when life has knocked us down, and managed to make everyone laugh (or at least crack a smile) through it all.

If the Girls are an ever-present wheel in my life, Elise is one of our spokes. She's a force of nature—a fierce lawyer, compassionate mediator, savvy businesswoman, devoted partner, amazing mom to five incredible children, and an always dedicated friend. And she does it all with an unstoppable spirit. She is determined to make the most out of every day, every opportunity, every setback, every life lesson. She soaks up wisdom wherever she can find it, and writes it all down so she can share it with others.

That's where this book comes in. It is full of Elise's characteristic insight and warmth. "I wrote this book because I want to contribute to someone else's happiness," she says, and I sincerely believe *More* will do just that. Because as Elise explains in these pages, with the right habits and practices sustained over time, you can become happier, more grateful, and more optimistic about your life and future.

This book contains wisdom of all kinds: scientific data, personal anecdotes, inspiring quotes, and helpful tips. It's part textbook, part memoir, part workbook. It brings intention together with action. And through it all, Elise's voice shines out—encouraging, no-nonsense, and confident that you can do it. I know that voice well—I've picked up the phone more times than I can count to hear it and draw strength from it. And I'm so excited that voice is now available to everyone.

There's a lot about this book I admire. But there are two things in particular I want to highlight.

First, Elise believes that personal happiness is connected to serving others. "Give more," she writes (she devotes a whole chapter to it!). Give more, because it will fulfill you. Give more, because it will make you appreciate all you have. Give more, because once you start, you'll want to keep giving. Give more, because even if you don't think you have much to give, you do. And if you need ideas, Elise has a long list to help you get started.

In a world that can feel chaotic and frightening, the idea that our personal happiness is intrinsically linked to other people's well-being—that we can lift ourselves up, not by putting ourselves first, but by putting others ahead of us—is empowering, inspiring, and just plain right. And Elise can teach this because she lives it. No one gives more to those around her.

Second, Elise knows about the happiness-generating power of friendship. "Friendships really matter," she writes, and I couldn't agree more. Some friends are our rocks in hard times. Some connect us to other people and communities. Some push us to try new things and consider new points of view. Some do all this and more. And to have good friends, you need to be a good friend yourself—which means taking action. Too often, we coast along in our friendships, especially the long-standing ones. We stop going the extra mile. We don't always call these friends back, we don't listen as closely as we used to. But it's our oldest friendships that need the most care and attention. And if we forget that, we risk losing some of the most precious resources in our lives. Elise knows the importance of activating these connections in your life, and as with every topic she tackles, she has tips and checklists to help you do it.

This book is generous, intelligent, and heartfelt. And I'm not just saying that because it was written by one of my dearest friends. It's because Elise has one of the sharpest wits and warmest spirits I've ever encountered—and this book captures both.

For years, I've picked up the phone and called Elise whenever I needed a dose of her wisdom and humor. And often I've passed along her advice. When you have a friend like her, you want to share with others everything that person has shared with you. That's why this book is such a special gift. Reading it feels like sitting across the table on a sunny morning, a mug of tea in hand, catching up with an old friend. I'm so glad that Elise is sharing it with the world.

Sheryl Sandberg
COO of Facebook and founder of LeanIn.Org and OptionB.
Org
October 2020

Contents

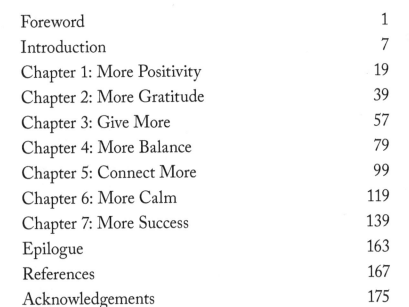

Introduction
More Happiness

For a long time it had seemed to me that life was about to begin, —real life. But there was always some obstacle in the way. Something to be got through first, some unfinished business, time still to be served, a debt to be paid.

–ALFRED D'SOUZA

When I was five years old, my mother always told me that happiness was the key to life. When I went to school, they asked me what I wanted to be when I grew up. I wrote down "happy." They told me I didn't understand the assignment, and I told them they didn't understand life.

–JOHN LENNON

At every stage of my life, I have anticipated the future. When I was younger, I had thoughts like *I can't wait to graduate; Just a few more years and I'll be living on my own; Soon I'll be married.* As I matured, my thoughts shifted: *In a few years the kids will be older and more self-sufficient; When I get that promotion I'll be content in my career; After I lose weight I'll feel better.* It has only been lately that I realized just how quickly life passes by. The quote "Happiness is a journey, not a destination" rings true—and it becomes more obvious to me the longer I live.

So, the question is, how do you avoid this constant looking forward to the future and make more out of your life *now*? I ask myself this all the time, as I strive to make more of the present. I have become determined to dig into the research and others' experience in order to really understand fulfillment and bring more to my life.

Happiness means different things to different people. Like everyone else, I have struggled with figuring out what true happiness looks like. Years ago, I started collecting anecdotes and life lessons to share with my children, nieces, and nephews as a way of helping them get through struggles, make the most of their lives, and learn how to be content. Eventually, I gathered enough information that it started to look like a book.

These life lessons and anecdotes—some large, some small, and some coming from the most unlikely sources—have helped me reevaluate my own life and what makes me happy. I don't claim to be an expert in happiness, but through my experiences and relationships, and by reading research in the field, I have learned an incredible amount that I want to share with others. As an attorney, mediator, business owner, consultant, volunteer, wife, and mother of five, I have seen many different interactions, emotions, struggles, and victories. I am blessed to be surrounded by a close-knit family and supportive friends who have taught me the importance of relationships, loyalty, and patience. The one common thread through it all is that I like to help people. I try to learn and grow from every encounter and then use the knowledge I have gained to help someone else. I wrote this book because I want to contribute to someone else's happiness. It is that simple.

These days, many authors, researchers, and psychologists are devoting substantial time and resources to finding the answer to what makes us happy. In the process, they've uncovered growing evidence that happiness can predict health and have a profound effect on the body—in fact, as much as environment and biology can.

A desire to understand happiness led to the creation of the annual *World Happiness Report* in 2012, which outlines the state of the world's happiness, including which countries fare better than others. (According to the 2019 *Happiness Report*, Finland is the happiest country in the world, with Denmark, Norway, Iceland, and the Netherlands rounding out the top five spots.) Each year, the report describes the issues connected to happiness, highlighting the importance of policies and ethics. Factors used to measure happiness levels include having someone to count on, the freedom to make key life decisions, generosity, and trust. Unsurprisingly, the report shows that people are happiest when they have strong social support and frequent meetings with friends.

Finding your happy

According to the research, you can control about 40 percent of your happiness. Of the rest, 10 percent is determined by your circumstances and 50 percent by your biology or genetics.

Dr. Sonja Lyubomirsky, a psychology professor and leading authority on happiness, theorizes that everyone has a set point from where they can either decrease or increase their happiness. What makes each of us happy is unique, and much of what we can control about our happiness level depends on our attitude, actions, and habits. Dr. Lyubomirsky has also investigated the various strategies you can use to be happy more often and even under difficult circumstances. Some of the strategies she has identified as effective include:

1. Regularly setting aside time to recall moments of gratitude (for example, by keeping a journal or writing gratitude letters);
2. Engaging in self-regulatory and positive thinking about yourself (such as by reflecting, writing, and talking about your happiest life events or goals for the future);
3. Practicing altruism and kindness (by routinely committing acts of kindness toward yourself and others);
4. Affirming your most important values (uncovering what really matters to you);
5. Savoring positive experiences (for example, by using your five senses to relish small, special moments during the day).

The key takeaway from her studies is this: *If you want to be happier, you need to work hard and take action to create good habits.* I have spent years struggling to incorporate these strategies into my own life; change does not happen overnight. I remember fixating on my children and work projects and struggling to find time to volunteer and participate in gratitude. I used and continue to use techniques like Dr. Lyubomirsky's and others that I mention throughout this book to help me improve on a daily basis. Just like everybody else, I have some days that are better than others. However, I can honestly say that this process has made me happier.

Small shifts in your mindset and perspective will make a big difference to your happiness when practiced regularly. Some techniques I have used include taking a few minutes each day to express gratitude, making more of an effort to see family and friends, and stop blaming others for my unhappiness. I have also tried to surround myself with people who inspire me, and although it's difficult at times, I try to resist the temptation to control, criticize, and judge others. Eliminating negativity in this way has positively impacted my own happiness and mindset.

Bringing more happiness into your life

Swiss psychiatrist Carl Jung was one of the first psychologists to discuss happiness in depth. He famously stated that "it all depends on how we look at things, and not how they are in themselves." Jung developed a list of the five essential elements for a happy life. Although he first introduced these back in 1960, they still hold true today:

1. **Good physical and mental health.** Exercising, eating right, and sleeping well remain the most effective and important ways to take care of yourself.
2. **Good personal and intimate relationships.** Satisfying relationships make us happy and impact our overall health. Our family, friends, neighbors, and colleagues have the ability to make us feel content and satisfied.

3. **The faculty for perceiving beauty in art and nature.** In other words, stop and smell the roses. Take time out from your busy life and go for a walk, participate in an outdoor activity, read a book, or listen to music— anything that allows you to see the beauty in the world around you.

4. **Reasonable standards of living and satisfactory work.** When we are feeling comfortable, safe, and productive, our levels of happiness go up.

5. **A philosophic or religious point of view capable of coping successfully with the vicissitudes of life.** Formal religion is not necessary to lead a happy life, but Jung believed that having something bigger than yourself to believe in could lead you down a path of happiness.

In 1938, Harvard began the Harvard Study of Adult Development, following participants for their entire lives to uncover what makes them happier, healthier, and live longer. George Vaillant, a former professor at Harvard Medical School led the study for more than thirty years. His book *Aging Well: Surprising Guideposts to a Happier Life from the Landmark Study of Adult Development* offered many insights from the study that can make our lives better, including many within our immediate control such as investing in relationships, improving our coping skills, and giving back to others and our community.

The interest in happiness continues to grow. The most popular class in Yale University's history is Psychology and the Good Life taught by Professor Laurie Santos. She created the course to respond to concerning levels of anxiety, stress, and depression among the student body. It gained such a following that she now offers an online class, The Science of Well-Being, which teaches students how to be happier using insights from psychology and techniques they can apply in real life.

Be the change you want to see

Over the last few years, I've collected articles and insights that have allowed me to bring more happiness into my life. I strive to live in the moment, whether working, spending time with family or friends, or enjoying a hobby. It is difficult to reach your full potential or appreciate the moment, whether good or bad, when your mind or emotions are somewhere else. No guilt can change the past and no amount of anxiety can alter the future. As Mark Twain said, "Worrying is like paying a debt you don't owe." If you find yourself struggling in your effort to grab hold of happiness, try focusing first on one aspect of your life that you can improve. Sometimes the simple act of just trying to improve yourself or your situation can bring about a great deal of satisfaction and happiness itself.

As you read through this book, choose one action each week and see how you can bring more into your life where it matters most. The next step is to stop blaming others and take responsibility for your own life and happiness. Avoid making excuses, stop complicating matters, and just be more.

The action you choose should contribute to your long-term happiness, not just your short-term happiness. Doing drugs, going on shopping sprees, drinking alcohol, and overindulging in video games can bring a quick jolt of pleasure, but it doesn't last. You build long-term happiness by spending time with family and friends, giving back to the community, and engaging in activities that foster more spirituality, faith, peace, and tranquility. Positive actions that contribute to your goals and dreams and improve your physical and mental health are what will bring you long-term happiness and fulfilment.

As I grow older, I often find myself doubting that I can change or add something different to my story. That's when I remind myself of Benjamin Franklin's words: "Change is the only constant in life. One's ability to adapt to those changes determines one's success." Things will change around us, but we can change too. It requires work, skill, determination, passion, and a commitment to using our experiences and our knowledge to make the right decisions to keep moving forward.

By changing your own habits, you can also impact others. Michelle Gielan and Shawn Achor are married researchers who research happiness around the world. In their 2017 article "The Science of Changing Other People: Positive Psychology Guides the Way to a Happiness Ripple Effect," they discussed how choosing to communicate an optimistic, empowered mindset to the people around you, especially in the face of adversity, drives positive outcomes. An optimistic mindset is infectious, and it lays the groundwork for individual and collective success. They counsel that "it is important to prime your day for success by knowing what kind of information is positively fueling you. Many things in this world are beyond your control. The problem occurs when you start to believe that *all* things are beyond your control—and that helpless mindset transfers to your work and relationships."

A good life is not out of your reach. It may take some effort, but achieving it is in your control. Throughout this book I will introduce actions you can implement right now to take that control. You can ask for help, live in the moment, express gratitude, prioritize your tasks, look for solutions, and plan pockets of enjoyment for yourself and your friends. These are small actions with big rewards; just a slight shift in mindset and consistent practice can bring significantly more happiness into your days.

Everyone can take a small step to improve their lives and be happier. So treasure every moment. Stop waiting until you lose weight, you have kids, your kids leave home, you start work, retire, get married, or pay your home off—there is no better time than right now to be happy and get more out of life.

Why More?

Years ago, a friend graciously wrote these words to me on my birthday:

> How do I define you? I came up with one word: more. Every time you rise, you give more, every time you give of yourself, you give more, every time someone asks for help, you are there to give more. Elise Scheck Bonwitt, if everyone around you is applauding you on this birthday week, it's because YOU truly define what we know is needed MORE of in the world. You exemplify goodness, kindness, sympathy, and we all know—action! More and more action each time! Words are meaningless without more action.

I knew when I received her kind words that if I ever organized my thoughts and research into a book, I would call it *More*, because I sincerely do want to make more of my life and have more impact every single day.

I have written *More* to be a simple resource on why and how to make small but meaningful life changes. As I gathered my thoughts and the research and quotes I had collected, I thought about the overall themes that had helped me improve my own life: positivity, gratitude, generosity, balance, relationships, calm, and success. It seemed natural that these topics should become the chapters to this book. Working to have more in these areas can help you in any facet of your life.

Even if you take just a few of the action steps in these pages, I will have accomplished my mission. Writing this book has been cathartic for me and has helped me improve where I was falling short, including connecting more with friends and showing more gratitude. It has made me feel increasingly content with what I have achieved so far and provided direction on how to set my goals for the future.

However you are feeling right now, whether it is stressed, stuck, or uninspired, this book will guide you through the steps toward change. Once you take action, you'll have the knowledge, habits, and energy to be happier. Life is always challenging, and every day your intentions, mood, resolve, values, and character will be tested. This book is meant to simplify your life by providing uncomplicated and straightforward information and tools to help you move forward and make the most of it.

Ask yourself, What do I believe in? What makes me happy? Who makes me happy? What is possible?

Answer these questions, make the changes you need, and be MORE.

THOUGHTS AND ACTIONS TOWARD MORE HAPPINESS

What are your happiest memories?

What events do you look forward to the most?

Who makes you happy?

Write down three action steps you will schedule on your calendar:
Some ideas include establishing a daily affirmation ritual, reaching out to a friend to make plans, visiting a special place, taking steps toward a goal, and planning a special celebration.

1.

2.

3.

MORE THOUGHTS

CHAPTER 1

More Positivity

Life changes very quickly, in a very positive way, if you let it.

–LINDSEY VONN

Resolve to keep happy, and your joy and you shall form an invincible host against difficulties.

–HELEN KELLER

Only through experience of trial and suffering can the soul be strengthened, ambition inspired, and success achieved.

–HELEN KELLER

I looked at social media one morning and the first thing I saw was a quote that a friend had posted: *Be the reason someone smiles today*. I was struck by how this comment exudes positivity and wondered: what positive thoughts can I put out into the world each day?

Each morning, we get to choose how we are going to perceive the world and what kind of impact we're going to have on others. Will you see the glass as half full or half empty? Will you look to the good that can happen that day, or will you assume that something will go wrong? Choosing to be positive can have a deep, beneficial effect on your life and the lives of those around you. Exposing yourself to negative people, negative news, or negative information can have the opposite result. You can choose to say no to things that are burdensome, stressful, and negative. You can choose not to say negative things about other people, not to get involved in drama between friends and colleagues.

When I think of positive affirmations, I laugh as I'm reminded of the character Stuart Smalley played by comedian Al Franken on *Saturday Night Live*, in a segment called "Daily Affirmations with Stuart Smalley." Smalley would look in a full-length mirror and say things like "I deserve good things," "I am entitled to my share of happiness," "I refuse to beat myself up," "I am an attractive person," or "I am fun to be with." He would give himself a pep talk and say, "I'm going to do a terrific show today! And I'm gonna help people! Because I'm good enough, I'm smart enough, and doggone it, people like me!"

Yes, we were supposed to laugh at Stuart, but there is some truth behind Franken's humor. Maybe we should all place inspirational notes on our mirrors and start the day with a verbal affirmation. Inside my medicine cabinet, I taped up a picture of my kids, a quote, and a prayer. The quote, written by Louise Hay, is "Whenever I encounter a challenge in my life, I use the experience to learn and grow." The prayer includes my thanks for good health, strength, community, food, shelter, and the wisdom to confront any difficulties that might come my way. I look at these things every morning and feel inspired. I also have taped quotes in different places around my office. Where's the first place you go each morning? The bathroom? Your closet? Your kitchen? Wherever it is, place an inspirational note or quote there, so you begin your day with a reminder of how you want to experience it and what you want to accomplish.

Being positive means figuring out ways to be inspired, taking control of your life, and accepting some responsibility. Focus on your mental, spiritual, and physical health. Choose hobbies, activities, and environments that you know will put you in a positive mood. Enroll in an exercise class, sign up for a sports league, read a book, paint, cook, or join a dance group. Come up with something, anything, that will improve your positivity. If you are on your way to work, think of something new you can learn there, an exciting project, or a colleague you would like to reach out to. Whether you decide to pursue a new hobby or activity—alone or with a friend—or change the way you approach your job, vow to bring more positivity into your life and then make it happen. Choose how you will live each day and be thoughtful and intentional about your actions and words.

Take small positive steps every day

It is difficult to be positive all the time, and we all have negative thoughts and feelings. When you do, make sure to treat yourself like a friend. Ask yourself, What would I be telling a friend under similar circumstances? What advice would I be giving them? This is a way to challenge your negative thoughts. Ask yourself further questions to uncover what your negative feelings are based upon. Challenging your own thinking, whether by examining it internally, discussing it with a friend, or writing about it in a journal, can be a big step toward enjoying a more positive outlook on life.

A friend recently told me that she struggled with negativity and would often spin out scenarios in her head that focused on her troubles and insecurities. For years, this left her exhausted and unable to move forward. After discussing her concerns with friends and a therapist, she learned how to retrain her thinking. She now knows how to replace negative thoughts with positivity. Over time, this change has made her a happier person who focuses on having a positive impact on others.

Positivity is a choice. Any happiness that is brought into your life depends on your outlook and attitude, and choosing to see things optimistically can have a profound effect on every aspect of your day. An essential part of getting more from life is bringing positivity to different situations and inspiring others to do the same. It is not always easy—in fact, it can often be a real struggle.

But sometimes, making even a tiny change can turn your mood around. It can be a small thing like adjusting your ringtone, listening to your favorite song, watching an old video, or even getting a haircut. When I wake up in a bad mood, I lift my spirits by putting on an inspiring piece of clothing or jewelry or, better yet, calling a friend or colleague to express gratitude or give a compliment. After a long and frustrating mediation where I am unable to help the parties resolve their differences, I get in my car and call a friend to catch up. After an argument with my husband, I unwind by reading a book. Other times, you may need a bigger change like enrolling in a class, volunteering at a shelter, ramping up your recycling, or even looking for a new job. Whatever your changes, no matter how small or how large, it always feels good when you are finally heading in the right direction. This is the key to leading a more positive and fulfilling life. Taking the first step—and the next and the next—can be difficult and frightening, but each little step can make a big difference.

As I mentioned, one of my favorite simple actions is showing appreciation to someone else. Did your partner or spouse make you coffee? Did you co-worker finish an assignment for you? Did a friend drop off the cup of sugar you needed? Did your kids stay quiet while you spent an extra half hour in bed? Showing any kind of appreciation, even for the small things, can help change your mood and set you up for a rewarding day.

A bigger positive step you can take is to help someone else. Give to a friend, a stranger, or an organization that is serving a greater purpose. Being altruistic can immediately attract more positivity. Consider volunteering at a school, shelter, park, or anywhere in your community that is doing good. Helping an organization or another person will allow you to focus on someone else, gain clarity regarding your own issues, and put the negativity aside.

Stay positive, stay healthy

A positive mindset is also good for your body. By becoming more positive and creating a better outlook on life, you will contribute not just to your mental health, but to your physical health as well. The American Institute of Stress estimates that stress-related problems are the cause of 75 to 90 percent of all visits to primary care physicians in the United States.

Lisa R. Yanek, MPH, and her colleagues at the Johns Hopkins University School of Medicine conducted a study connecting positivity and health that was published in the *American Journal of Cardiology*. The study included 1,483 healthy people with siblings who had experienced some sort of coronary event (including heart attack and sudden cardiac death) before the age of sixty. The study participants periodically filled out surveys about their well-being, life satisfaction, relaxation levels, anxiety levels, cheerful mood, and level of health concern. Yanek and her colleagues followed up with the participants after an average of twelve years and found that there had been 208 coronary events. Overall, they discovered that positive people were less likely than their negative counterparts to have a heart attack or other coronary event—even those with a family history of cardiac disease and the most risk factors. In fact, after controlling for cardiac risk factors, having positive well-being was linked with a one-third reduction in coronary events—and among those who were most likely to experience a coronary event, positive well-being was linked with an almost 50 percent reduction.

As research continues in this area, I suspect that that further links between physical health and positive emotions—including happiness, fulfillment, the ability to relax, and lower anxiety levels—will come to light.

Spread the word

Whenever I pass through the airport on the way back from a trip, I buy my husband a "Life is Good" shirt, a simple act of positivity that has grown into a loving habit over the years.

More than three decades ago, the Jacobs brothers started the business Life is Good. Bert Jacobs is now the chief executive optimist of the $100 million company. Their goal was to spread happiness to others throughout the world. Their secret weapon? Positivity.

Things didn't start out so rosy. In 1994, after five years of selling T-shirts out of their car to college students, the Jacobs brothers had less than stellar sales and just seventy-eight dollars left to their names. In response, they decided to add an optimistic message to their shirts. They designed their first "Life is Good" T-shirt and discovered how those three simple words could help people focus on the positive. Those three words also turned their business around. According to their website, "Optimism isn't irrational cheerfulness, and it's not blind positivity. It's a powerful approach to accomplishing goals and living a fulfilling life. By acknowledging obstacles and opportunities—but focusing on the opportunities— optimism enables us to explore the world with open arms and an eye toward solutions and growth. It also makes life a hell of a lot more fun."

Peace Love World is another apparel business that became successful by putting out positive messages. Alina Villasante, the founder and designer of this lifestyle brand, has become an advocate for inspiring others to be their best self. In 2009, Alina started her company with the idea of spreading positive affirmations after she realized that everyone was starving for peace, love, and happiness. She used her brand to spread her message. I received one of Alina's bags labeled "Choose Happiness" as a gift. It makes me smile whenever I use it. Her apparel and accessories have since been sold in more than two thousand boutiques and major retailers around the world. According to her website, Alina's destiny is "always keeping the light on even in the dark."

A popular spinning instructor in Miami and Toronto sells shirts with different inspiring messages including "Blessed," "Never Give Up," "Rise Up," "Warrior," "Better Together," and "This Is Me." She does not just sell shirts to brand her name; she does it to spread positivity among her clients and friends (I am lucky to be one of them) and throughout her community.

Positive messages are all around us. They can be heard, seen, and felt by millions, through pop culture and other channels. You can accept and be inspired by these messages every day. One of my favorite songs is "You Gotta Be" by Des'ree. It is the perfect tune to belt out to when you need to take yourself to another level. Irish band The Script motivate their audiences to never give up when they sing "Hall of Fame." And Alicia Keys' powerful ballad "Girl on Fire" can give anyone the power and inspiration to take the next step forward. Whenever I'm feeling down, I can turn on one of these songs and it will shift my entire day. And I'm not the only one; in a 2019 Verywell Mind article, Kendra Cherry cites research that shows that music can boost a person's mood, make them happier, and reduce anxiety. We all need inspiration at times to turn the negative into a positive and be motivated to shine that light onto others.

Music, art, sports, and other hobbies or activities can have positive effects on your health. The ability to give positive experiences to yourself and others will lead to more confidence and many other health benefits.

Be a solutionist

I have always told my children to surround themselves with positive people, since research tells us that you become like the ten people you spend the most time with. Jim Rohn, an entrepreneur, author, and motivational speaker stated that "you are the average of the five people you spend the most time with." Eliminating negativity from your life can literally save your life, while surrounding yourself with negative people can waste precious energy and contribute to stress, anxiety, and high blood pressure. Studies have shown that negativity can even rewire your brain, making it easier to see the bad in the world and harder to see the good.

According to Dr. Travis Bradberry, co-author of *Emotional Intelligence 2.0*, repeated complaining rewires your brain to make future complaining more likely. Over time, you find it is easier to be negative than to be positive, regardless of what's happening around you. Complaining becomes your default behavior. It damages other areas of your brain as well; research from Stanford University has shown that complaining shrinks the hippocampus—an area of the brain that's critical to problem solving and intelligent thought.

Positivity is a muscle that grows with use, and with practice it can create a happier and healthier life. Bringing optimism into your day will only make things better. Focus your energy on positive things, even when times are tough. Focus on solutions instead of problems. A word I created years ago is "solutionist." When one of my children got stuck on a project for school, instead of solving the problem for them, I would tell them to become a solutionist, asking them to think positively about the steps necessary to accomplish it. Becoming a solutionist not only helps you solve problems but also makes you more confident, successful, and optimistic. Focusing on solutions can help you remain positive. Have you ever noticed that it is usually the negative co-worker or friend who complains when they have to fix something? When you become more positive, problems become opportunities, and success comes your way.

There's no denying that becoming an optimistic person can be challenging. If you look, you can always find something bad going on in your personal life, your community, or somewhere in the world. We are living in especially turbulent and unpredictable times right now. Just turn on the news or read the paper and you will find many troubling stories that could easily shatter your mood, hopes, and dreams. It is important to remember that even negative experiences or people can lead to a more positive situation by giving you a lesson you need or an opportunity to learn. To move past the negativity, you have to define your purpose and focus on solutions, your strengths, and your accomplishments. Avoid ruminating over perceived failures—keep your focus on what is working instead of what is not. That's what will let you turn those problems into opportunities. That's when you turn into a solutionist.

The power of positive psychology

The term "positive psychology" was originally coined by the psychologist Abraham Maslow in the 1950s. Martin Seligman, who popularized the concept through his influential 2002 work *Authentic Happiness*, spent his entire career researching positivity and the impact it has on our lives. He defined positive psychology as the study of positive emotions and the "strengths that enable individuals and communities to thrive." In his book, he discusses the concept's three pillars: positive emotions, positive individual traits, and positive institutions. Understanding positive emotions entails the study of contentment with the past, happiness in the present, and hope for the future.

Researcher Courtney E. Ackerman recently wrote an article for *Positive Psychology* magazine that discussed what a positive mindset is and ways we can achieve it. She states that "positivity doesn't always refer to simply smiling and looking cheerful . . . positivity is more about one's overall perspective on life and their tendency to focus on all that is good in life." She shares the definition of positive mindset according to Kendra Cherry at Verywell Mind: "Positive thinking actually means approaching life's challenges with a positive outlook. It does not necessarily mean avoiding or ignoring the bad things; instead, it involves making the most of the potentially bad situations, trying to see the best in other people, and viewing yourself and your abilities in a positive light." Basically, it's focusing on the bright side, expecting positive results, and approaching challenges with an optimistic outlook.

Throughout their books and articles, Ackerman, Seligman, and many others share their advice on ways to achieve more positivity. A few of my favorite positive actions include using positive affirmations, placing inspirational quotes around my home and office, writing down my thoughts in a journal, texting or emailing a positive message to someone I care about, focusing on the good things that happened to me throughout the day, and using humor in appropriate situations. If I'm feeling down, I try to watch a funny video or TV show or spend time with a positive person. I try to see the silver lining and smile at every opportunity.

We all have the power to turn negativity into positivity, and by taking small steps, you can train yourself to have an optimistic mindset. For many, a good place to start is by paying more attention to the words you use. Do any of the following phrases sound familiar? *I can't. I won't accomplish anything. I don't have the time. I have the worst luck.* Be on the lookout for negative phrases, complaints, or expletives that you say often and work on replacing them with something more positive. Focus on starting your day with positive speech. Instead of saying "I can't" maybe you can say "Today is the day I can try to accomplish my goals" or "Today is the day I will make that call" or "Today will be a great day" or "Today I will try to brighten up my friend's life."

It is important to recognize that even negative experiences or people can lead to a more positive situation by teaching you something. In his book *Positive Intelligence*, Shirzad Chamine discusses his Three-Gifts technique, which is a tactic for finding the positive in negative situations. He suggests that every time you encounter a bad situation, think of three scenarios in which the situation is actually a good thing. You can also decide to "just let it go and put it behind you without any residue of unhappiness, regret, or distress. . . . Ironically, deciding to just let a negative situation go rather than actively turn it into a gift is a gift in itself: you're strengthening the muscle that allows you to let go of regret, guilt, or shame."

Always look for the good

Another way to train your brain to be more optimistic is by remembering, photographing, recording, or writing down the positive events in your day. Recently, my children were playing a game together, either Catan or Codenames, and it made me happy, so I took a picture. I know when I'm feeling down or missing them, I will look at that photograph and it will make me smile. If you had a particularly good day at work, at home, or elsewhere, write about it in your journal or make a note on your mobile phone or computer. (When I need to capture something right away, I use the notes app on my phone so I don't forget.) If you pass a particularly beautiful area, take a picture or make a note. If you have attended an interesting class or conference or had a productive meeting, keep a record of the highlights. As you take note of the positive that surrounds you on a daily basis, you will be training yourself to look for it, which helps you become more optimistic. There are times when this may not be easy, but you can train yourself to see at least one positive thing on even the darkest day.

As you begin to practice optimism, make it a point to avoid drama and negativity. You may not be able to escape all of it, but you can control some of it. For example, if you find yourself viewing negative videos, channels, and social media, STOP. Instead, read a book, call a friend, or do an errand. Filling your head with constant negativity is only going to produce a more negative mindset.

To bring more positivity into your life, be thoughtful about how often you smile. Try to make someone else smile. When you pass a stranger at the market, just smile. There have been studies that show that the act of smiling alone can improve your mood. Giving a compliment has the same effect, with the extra bonus of making the other person smile. So, if you like a blouse that a friend is wearing, tell them. If you like the project that a co-worker just completed, tell them. If you like the food and service at a restaurant, tell them. If you like the shoes that a stranger is wearing, tell them. You'll not only give someone else a boost, but you will contribute to your overall positive mindset too.

The book *The Last Lecture* is based on a talk given by Randy Pausch in September 2007 titled "Really Achieving Your Childhood Dreams." Pausch, a professor at Carnegie Mellon, delivered his last lecture about a month after he was given the diagnosis of terminal pancreatic cancer. During the lecture, he was upbeat and humorous, shrugging off the pity often given to people with a terminal illness. At one point during the lecture, he actually dropped down and did push-ups onstage.

Despite his terminal illness, he was determined to spread positivity to his students and community. At the end of his lecture he makes this very meaningful point: "It's not about how to achieve your dreams. It's about how to lead your life. If you lead your life the right way, the karma will take care of itself. The dreams will come to you."

Pausch's book became a *New York Times* bestseller in 2008 and remained on the list for 112 weeks. It has been translated into forty-eight languages and has sold millions of copies throughout the word. His video has been watched by hundreds of thousands of people searching for positive messages. His strength and positivity inspired them all to think about what really matters and to energize others to affirm life by relentlessly pursuing their dreams.

Pausch is a perfect example of what to do when bad things happen. Even with his terminal prognosis, he chose to bring positivity into his own life and the lives of others. I am sure he had bad days, but he figured out ways to spread a positive message on his good days. He could have given up, but instead he focused on the things that he could control, like his message to his students and colleagues.

I have always told my friends and family that they should celebrate milestones. When someone tells me that they are going to skip their birthday, I insist that they should never miss an opportunity to observe the occasion with their loved ones. Several months ago, I invited my female friends and family to celebrate my fiftieth birthday at a camp in North Carolina. I was determined to create a positive experience for the most important women in my life. We slept in cabins, hiked, participated in color war, ate in the dining hall, sang around the campfire, danced, and laughed together. A lot.

Make positivity a habit

Anyone—even someone who is naturally negative—can become more positive; just a few changes every day can create new habits. You need to remind yourself that even though bad things happen, life can turn around. At the beginning of the week, write down one thing you can do each day to make things a little better, like sending positive emails, praising the people in your life, and celebrating milestones. Make a list of your blessings and try to spend time with people who make you happy.

Many people are so busy with work and keeping up with their families that they don't make positivity and optimism a priority. If you have a hard time seeing the good in people and accepting that life is cyclical, sit down and make a list of all your blessings. Then focus on sharing one of these blessings with someone else. For example, if you are blessed with an abundance of food, share this blessing by donating some of it to a homeless shelter. Many years ago, despite my busy schedule with work and family, I decided to spend one hour every weekend taking my son to a homeless shelter to serve food to its residents. This simple act of service taught him how to bring positivity to others despite whatever problems he had. It has not always been easy to find this time to volunteer. I made it a priority, put it in my calendar, and discussed the idea with my children. Once I put the idea out for discussion, I knew I had to follow through.

Schedule a few minutes every day to celebrate or plan your next milestone or accomplishment, reach out to a friend and give positive praise, or simply be proud of one of your accomplishments by sharing it with at least one other person. Choose your words wisely, never talk about the failings of others, and try to see the good in everyone. Be mindful during your conversations with others and try to talk with positivity. If there's something bad going on in your life, share it, but also include at least one good thing in the conversation too. Try to radiate a positive and renewable energy that will not only promote what is positive in your life but will raise others up with you.

Many people believe that habits are formed by performing a task for twenty-one days in a row; some research has found it can take up to sixty-six days, or even a year. Whatever the case may be, it is important to start building that habit by committing yourself to at least one positive action a day. Eventually, you will find yourself automatically including a positive action in each day—and most likely more.

SEVEN ACTION STEPS TO CREATE MORE POSITIVITY

1. Start your day with a positive affirmation.

2. Keep quotes and sayings in key locations to lift your spirits.

3. Contact or make plans with someone in your social circle who builds you up.

4. Do one thing that brings you joy, whether it's putting on a favorite shirt, listening to your favorite song, or reading a good book.

5. Write down one or more things you are grateful for. Attitude is everything, and being grateful makes a huge difference.

6. Send encouraging words to a family member, friend, or colleague.

7. Take one step toward pursuing your goals.

THOUGHTS AND ACTIONS TOWARD MORE POSTIVITY

When do you feel the most positive?

How do you create positive energy?

Who is the most positive person in your life?

Write down three action steps you will schedule on your calendar:
Some ideas include creating daily affirmations, starting a journal, giving at least one compliment a day, smiling more, and focusing energy on positive things.

1.

2.

3.

MORE THOUGHTS

_____

_____

_____

_____

_____

_____

_____

_____

_____

_____

_____

_____

CHAPTER 2

More Gratitude

Enjoy the little things, for one day you may look
back and realize they were the big things.

–ROBERT BRAULT

Gratitude . . . turns what we have into enough,
and more. It turns denial into acceptance, chaos
to order, confusion to clarity. . . . Gratitude makes
sense of our past, brings peace for today, and
creates a vision for tomorrow.

–MELODY BEATTIE

There was a world-famous painter who in the prime of her
career started losing her eyesight. Fearful that she might no
longer be able to paint, she went to see the best eye surgeon

in the world. After a delicate surgery and several weeks of therapy, her eyesight was restored. The painter decided to show her gratitude by decorating the doctor's office. Part of her work included painting a gigantic eye on one wall. When she had finished, she held a press conference to unveil her work of art. One reporter noticed the eye on the wall and asked the doctor, "What was your first reaction upon seeing your newly painted office, especially that large eye on the wall?" To this, the eye doctor responded, "I said to myself, 'Thank heavens I'm not a proctologist.'"

A funny joke, but the message is serious. Whether you paint a mural, write a card, send an email, or make a call, there are always ways to use your talents and resources to show gratitude. Each year there are scores of appreciation days to celebrate different groups: Teacher Appreciation Day, International Friendship Day, National Good Neighbor Day, National Nurses Day, Senior Citizens Day—the list goes on. Wouldn't it be even better if these days weren't necessary, if people felt appreciated all year round?

Gratitude is one of the simplest ways to get more out of life. Bringing more gratitude into your life can foster improved relationships, increased self-esteem, and even better health. Throughout history, societies have noticed the benefits of gratitude. More than two thousand years ago, Marcus Tullius Cicero, a Roman philosopher and statesman, wrote, "Gratitude is not only the greatest of virtues, but the parent of all others." More recently, the Holocaust survivor Israel Joe Sachs taught our family about the virtue of gratitude. He survived several concentration camps and suffered the most unimaginable horrors at the hands of the Nazis. Despite the sorrow, tragedies, and heavy burdens he endured, he always was grateful for his family and friends, and for his ability to share his story and inspire others. His gratitude does not express denial but comes from his recognition that there is always hope and goodness even in our darkest moments.

The health benefits of gratitude are widely known among researchers. Several studies have linked gratitude to lowered stress, decreased aggression, and improvements in impulse control. One such study by Roland Zahn and colleagues from the National Institutes of Health (2009) examined blood flow in various brain regions while subjects summoned up feelings of gratitude. They found that subjects who showed more gratitude overall had higher levels of activity in the hypothalamus, the area of the brain that controls a vast array of essential bodily functions, including eating, drinking, and sleeping. It also has a huge influence on your metabolism and stress levels. It starts to become clear how increased feelings of gratitude could have such wide-ranging beneficial effects—from improved sleep to decreased depression and much more.

Gratitude can also benefit your mental health and well-being. Using MRI images, neuroscientists discovered that the same regions of the brain associated with socialization and pleasure light up when you experience gratitude.

Robert A. Emmons, PhD, a professor of psychology at the University of California, Davis, has been nicknamed the "father of gratitude." He has written several books and more than one hundred articles on gratitude, as well as being the editor in chief of *The Journal of Positive Psychology*. Emmons's extensive research has uncovered numerous ways for people to use gratitude to significantly improve their health and well-being. In a 2003 study, Emmons and his colleague Michael McCullough investigated how gratitude affects psychological and physical well-being. They found that practicing gratitude can have a positive impact across almost every aspect of your life and that journaling daily can increase overall well-being, reduce health issues, and create a more optimistic outlook.

During an interview, Emmons described gratitude as "an affirmation of the goodness in one's life and the recognition that the sources of this goodness lie at least partially outside the self. It emerges from two-stages of information processing: affirming and recognizing. Gratitude is the recognition that life owes me nothing and all the good I have is a gift. It is a response to all that has been given. So it is foundationally and fundamentally a way of looking at life."

He also described how many people suffer from "gratitude deficit disorder" due to a sense of entitlement, negative bias, need to be self-reliant, or preoccupation with the busyness of modern times. When asked if his research could benefit society, Emmons replied, "Gratitude has the power to heal, energize, and change our lives. It's not simply that gratitude brings more happiness or better health. It's much more than that. It literally breathes new life into us! And society needs more people who are alive."

The many benefits of gratitude

The research, confirmed by my own personal experience, makes it clear that gratitude is good for us. If you express gratitude regularly, your stress levels will be lower, your relationships will be improved, and you will be happier. This is no longer anecdotal; it's been proven time and again by researchers all over the world.

Gratitude can also increase self-confidence, because you are content with what you have and are less likely to compare yourself to others. You will pay less attention to what others have, especially material objects, when you live your life with more gratitude. Jealousy will not arise when you are satisfied with your possessions and, more importantly, your social circles. When jealousy is not a factor, you can foster better relationships with family members, friends, and colleagues. This will impact your personal and professional experiences and accomplishments.

More gratitude also reduces toxic emotions and improves overall physical health. Moments of gratitude stick with us and contribute to special memories and enjoyable relationships. The surprising thing about gratitude is that it actually helps you just as much (sometimes even more) than the person you're expressing your gratitude toward. When you feel grateful, you will want less and be more satisfied with where you are and what you already have in life.

Acknowledging the good that is already in your life is the foundation for all abundance.
–ECKHART TOLLE

Practicing gratitude can have a long-lasting and positive impact on our lives and health in ways that many of us don't fully realize. For example, there is a remarkable correlation between gratitude and increased longevity and improved health. Growing evidence indicates that gratitude interventions result in greater life satisfaction, more patience, more self-control, optimism, and enhanced overall well-being. In May 2018, the Greater Good Science Center at UC Berkeley reviewed the individual and social benefits of gratitude, finding that it improved our health, happiness, and relationships.

Expressing gratitude in daily life

It's clear that being grateful is beneficial to your health and well-being, as well as to those around you. So how can you bring more of it into your life? Showing gratitude is much more than a simple "thanks" without further thought. To improve the quality of your life and the lives of others, it is important to show true gratitude for the things you are thankful for and let the people in your life know just how much you appreciate them. "When we are truly grateful, we tend to look for ways to demonstrate it, along with love or affection," says Talkspace therapist Cynthia Catchings. "We also have to remember the law of attraction. When we are grateful, we invite the universe to manifest more of what we like, need, or enjoy."

Gratitude is the reason that thousands of families look forward to celebrating Thanksgiving and participating in traditions that express gratitude to those who are closest to them. These are times when we all stop, take notice of the little things that are important in life, and appreciate such special moments. But why can't we show this kind of gratitude all year long? Why can't we exhibit these feelings every day?

There are countless ways to integrate regular expressions of gratitude into your everyday life, including just showing up for the important moments, large and small. Some families write notes to one another, while others give speeches at Thanksgiving to everybody about all the things they are grateful for. I have family who go around the table for every birthday and ask every person what they are grateful for. On a birthday, or just for no reason at all, you can send a card to express your gratitude for a friend or family member. I keep a box of cards that I received over the years from my children, husband, family, and friends. When I need inspiration and a reminder of why I should be grateful, I read one of them. I am not only reminded of why I should be grateful, but it inspires me to show gratitude to others. I have a T-shirt that says, "Be grateful," and I wear it whenever I'm feeling down because it reminds me of all the things and people that I'm thankful for.

One of my favorite objects is a book by Charlie Harary called *Unlocking Greatness* that my son gave me two years ago. It contains an inscription from my son describing his gratitude for his upbringing and the many things I have done for him over the years. This book is now one of my most treasured possessions. Seems like a small gesture, but it had an enormous impact on me. Not only did I feel appreciated, but it was one of the catalysts that gave me the courage to write this book.

One Mother's Day, my children gave me a jar full of notes, each stating a different reason they are grateful for having me as a mom. This is a simple, inexpensive, and effective way to show gratitude. It not only benefited the recipient (me) but also the givers. My kids were extremely proud and happy about their gift.

I received a similar jar from my college friends filled with notes describing what they appreciated about me and our relationships. A jar is an unremarkable item, but when you fill it with scraps of paper that say things like "Always has time for her friends" or "Gives great book recommendations" or "Believes that nothing is impossible" or "Makes me laugh" or "You give the best advice," it becomes the best gift ever. It sits on my bookshelf and inspires me to be better and show gratitude to others. I was thankful when I received the jar, but my college friends didn't know quite how much that jar means to me. They will now.

You never know when an expression of gratitude will change someone's life. A simple gesture can brighten someone else's day; it can also make your day more special. When life gets busy, sometimes it seems hard to show gratitude to others, but, if you set aside just a few minutes a day, you can always find some way to express real thanks. Sometimes just a simple text or call to show your gratitude can go a very long way. If there is enough time, you can use a grander gesture like a gift or card or surprise drop-by or huge shout-out on social media.

Here are some of my favorite ways to express gratitude:

- Send a handwritten thank-you card explaining how that person has changed your life. I mentor girls at a nearby high school, and one day I brought thank-you cards in so they could write to someone special in their lives—either a parent, teacher, or friend. They were excited to write the cards and even requested more. Not only were the girls happy for the lesson and opportunity to give thanks—the recipients of those cards were also thrilled.
- Whether you call, write a card, email, or text to give thanks, try to explain your appreciation in detail. Let someone know exactly why you are grateful to have them as a friend, colleague, neighbor, or family member. Give an example or a few examples of things they have done or said that gave you a boost.
- Offer to do something for a person who has done so much for you. If you know they need to pick something up, offer to run the errand for them. Let them know that you want to do the task in gratitude for something they have done for you.

- Give someone a hug! This is a proven and effective way to give thanks. I am not kidding; my son just gave me a hug and thanked me for something I did for him while I was writing this section. Nothing better than a hug.
- Buy a gift to show your gratitude. A small token of appreciation is always welcome, especially when it is not expected. If you see a small gift in a store that makes you think of someone, buy it for them if you can. Years ago, my cousin bought me a small tray inscribed "Cousins because our parents couldn't handle us as sisters" because it made her think of me; I still put my rings on it today because it makes me think of her.
- Spend time with others, especially during difficult moments. Plan a special day or night for someone to show your gratitude.
- Show it off—if someone buys you a gift, be sure to display it. You can wear a piece of clothing or jewelry that they bought for you. Display a gift they got you in your home, office, or business. I have seen many businesses with proudly framed and displayed dollar bills that were given to the owners when they first opened up.
- Give compliments and make them genuine.
- Surprise someone at their home or office with their favorite muffin, coffee, or flowers.
- Post it—leave sticky notes with grateful messages around their office or house.
- Cook/bake a favorite meal or snack for a family member or friend.
- Make a donation to a local charity in honor of someone special.

- Create a coupon booklet—my niece just told me about a booklet that my other niece gave her that included coupons for a free massage, free errand, and other fun little activities.
- Make a collage or video that showcases all the happy moments you shared with a friend. This can be for a birthday, a special celebration, congratulations for a big achievement or milestone, or just to say thanks.
- Craft a homemade thank-you. Take a picture of your family holding thank-you signs or other messages of gratitude. For years, I designed cards with my kids and sent them as holiday greetings with a note of appreciation to family and friends.
- Tip, compliment, and report on good service. A good tip shows how much good service is appreciated. You can also compliment your server and let their supervisors know about their excellent work. This can apply to many different industries—even when tipping is not appropriate, a compliment always is.
- Go online to merchants who make or sell objects you love and leave a positive review. The merchant (and the next shopper) will appreciate it.
- Write in a daily or weekly gratitude journal. Take a few moments each night or morning to write down the things you were grateful for that day or the day before. Appreciate the little things in life by writing them down.
- Always say thank you. No matter how small or how big the favor was, always say thank you. Say it to family, friends, co-workers, and strangers. I always try to say it to the person at the cash register at my supermarket or the person who holds the door for me at a store or

the teller at my bank. Get in the habit of saying thank you to everyone you interact with throughout the day. A thank-you can go a long way, and you never know when someone really needs to hear it.

- When appropriate, compliment someone at work or any organization that you are part of and tell them—in front of others—the reasons they are appreciated. Verbalize your thanks to that awesome co-worker. This can really make their day.

- Send notes to people on appreciation days. On your local teacher's appreciation day, have your child send a note of thanks to their teachers, administrators, and coaches.

- Show gratitude through social media. When appropriate, express thanks to people and businesses on Facebook, Instagram, Twitter, or wherever you post.

It's all in the details

In order for gratitude to work, there needs to be sincerity. Usually, that's found in the details. The more specific the act of gratitude, the more sincere it will feel. For example, when I tell my husband he is a good man, that is nice and shows some gratitude. However, if I tell him that I appreciate that he spent the day with our son, booked flights for our family, or that he did the dishes, my sentiments show more depth and gratitude. Gratitude in depth is more important than gratitude by the numbers. Taking this extra step will show authenticity, and your friends and family will recognize that you don't take them for granted. Although saying "Thanks for everything" is nice, imagine if you used words like "Thanks for the great dinner and conversation" or "Thanks for following up on that favor I asked of you." On a friend's birthday, don't just tell them that you are grateful for their friendship, tell them why and give a specific example like "I appreciate the great advice you gave me" or "I appreciate the time you picked up my children at school" or "I appreciate that you showed up at my house when you knew I was having a bad day." Elaborating on a particular event or detail can make that expression of gratitude so much more meaningful to your friend.

Feeling gratitude is a habit that can be learned. Because of the brain's inherent neuroplasticity, we have the power to train it to seek out moments of gratitude. This is good news for anyone who is worried that they will be stuck in a glass-half-empty mentality forever. With conscious practice, you have the ability to rewire your brain. Instead of defaulting to what's not working, you can learn to focus on what is, and be grateful for it.

There are several ways we can teach our kids to feel gratitude. As therapist Cynthia Catchings said, "We can teach our children to be mindful of their emotions and use positive thoughts that lead them to being grateful." When children learn to be mindful of who or what creates the positive aspects in their lives, they learn to appreciate what is given to them and what they have, instead of concentrating on what they don't.

To become a more grateful person, write down one thing that you are grateful for before you go to sleep and one thing you are excited about when you wake up. You can use a journal or save these moments in a notes app on your phone. During hard times this task can be difficult, but there should always be at least one thing you are grateful for—being alive, having your health, enjoying a great cup of coffee, or even just getting one thing done from your to-do list.

Another way to become more grateful is to commit to showing gratitude to at least one person each day, whether face-to-face or via a text, card, email, or call. If possible, try to schedule it for the same time every week. How great would it be to start every Monday with a gratitude message to someone in your life? That person does not always have to be an obvious choice. It could be a friend you haven't seen in years or a teacher who once inspired you to excel in a certain subject. You could send a letter to a doctor or nurse who helped you weather a medical crisis or to a friend who has been there for you through the good times and the bad. Not only can this make someone's day (if not week), but if you pay attention, you will notice that you are smiling while expressing your gratitude.

Be grateful every day

Even the busiest people can find at least one minute a day to show gratitude. Don't dismiss just saying thank you for the simple things. My friend bought a gratitude box for me years ago with a pen and paper inside. It prompts me to write down one thing I am grateful for each day. I also take the opportunity to write thank-you texts or letters or emails to people who have helped me along the way. Recently, my mother was in the hospital, and I had my daughter write a thank-you letter to the doctor who saved her life. Not only did this simple exercise allow my daughter to show gratitude, but it made the doctor's day too. There are countless ways you can show gratitude to family members, friends, and even strangers. I try not to miss these opportunities because you never know when it will make a difference to someone else.

MORE

If you have a difficult time coming up with what to write in a gratitude journal, go back to the basics. Some days, you can be grateful for the simple things in life, like health, nature, music, books, food, family, time, animals, seasons, shelter, peace, and love. Other times, you can be more specific. Is there a person who helped you today? Did you get some good news? Did you eat a great meal? Did you finish an assignment? Did you have a great conversation with an old friend? Did you hear from a relative? Did your health improve? If you pay attention, you will find that there is much in this world to be grateful for.

Gratitude is the healthiest of all human emotions. The more you express gratitude for what you have, the more likely you will have even more to express gratitude for.

–ZIG ZIGLAR

SEVEN ACTION STEPS TO CREATE MORE GRATITUDE

1. Schedule a time on your calendar once a week to send thank-you cards or e-messages for any reason. Try to send one to three a week.

2. Record in your journal, notepad, computer, or mobile phone one word a day that explains what you are grateful for. It can be a person, accomplishment, or feeling. Anything!

3. Start each morning by writing one thing in your journal that you are excited about for that day. It could be something you are doing, someone you are seeing, or even just the sunshine.

4. Give at least one gratitude gift or card a month. Schedule it in your calendar.

5. Aim to say thanks at every opportunity, to friends, family, people in your community, and even strangers. If someone helps you in even a small way, tell them it's appreciated.

6. Make it a habit to let the people in your life know how grateful you are for the things they do. Let them know whenever you have a chance.

7. When showing your appreciation, be specific about why. Telling someone exactly why you are grateful always means so much more than a general statement.

THOUGHTS AND ACTIONS
TOWARD MORE GRATITUDE

What are you grateful for in your life?

Whom are you grateful for in your life?

What are the little things you are grateful for?

Write down three action steps you will schedule on your calendar:
Some ideas include writing in a gratitude journal, writing a thank-you card or email once a week, and saying thank you to someone at least once a day.

1.

2.

3.

MORE THOUGHTS

MORE

_____

_____

_____

_____

_____

_____

_____

_____

_____

_____

_____

_____

_____

_____

CHAPTER 3

Give More

Only by giving are you able to receive more than you already have.

–JIM ROHN

No one has ever become poor from giving.

–ANNE FRANK

There is a Chinese saying that goes, "If you want happiness for an hour, take a nap. If you want happiness for a day, go fishing. If you want happiness for a month, get married. If you want happiness for a year, inherit a fortune. If you want happiness for a lifetime, help somebody." For centuries, the greatest thinkers have suggested the same thing: Happiness is found in helping others.

When you give more, you'll feel more fulfilled. Generosity not only makes us happier; it often has a ripple effect. The recipients appreciate and enjoy receiving from others, and many will end up paying it forward. As the giver, you'll feel good too—which is why when you witness an act of generosity, whether in person, on social media, or on television, you will usually see smiles on the faces of both the giver and the receiver.

There are endless opportunities to be generous with your time, words, connections, and resources. Whether I am giving or receiving, I can attest to the fact that it just feels good. Even when I am having a down day or not feeling right, I remind myself that there is always someone in a worse position—and I try to think of an opportunity to be generous to them.

When I need inspiration, or a reminder of why I give, I look at the quote I have hanging in my office: "Be the change you wish to see in the world." Every time you are kind and give to others, no matter how much or how little you can offer, it will spark a change. You are not only giving to someone else; you are initiating a reaction that will continue well beyond your initial act, like a cascade of dominoes. You may never know how far your kindness has reached. For example, many years ago I collected some hygiene products to donate to at-risk girls. Another person in my community heard about my project and was inspired to do her own drive and volunteer at a nearby shelter. It was years before I heard about the positive impact my actions had sparked in her.

Why giving makes you happy

Generosity can even help you when you are going through a difficult time. Years ago, my son was diagnosed with

APMPPE, a rare eye disorder. Thankfully, his vision has not been drastically impaired, but for several months before his diagnosis, we were told that there was a significant probability that he would lose his sight completely. What helped me through this time was learning about the visually impaired community, doing research, and giving back to the Miami Lighthouse for the Blind. Becoming part of this wonderful support system helped me immensely at the time and enabled me to meet their CEO, Virginia Jacko. She is a remarkable human being who is blind herself and spends her days giving back to this incredible organization.

Generosity has a physical effect on both the giver and the receiver, so embrace your ability to give in every way possible. Pay more compliments, reach out to friends and colleagues with words of encouragement, and give your time, resources, and money whenever you have the opportunity.

When my children were younger, I spent time volunteering with them at several organizations in my community. We would stack shelves at a local food bank, paint dilapidated schools, donate items to families in need, and sign up for other volunteer projects that became available. It not only made my children aware of their surroundings and the needs of others, but it helped me fulfill and enhance my desire to help others too. Once I started giving more with my children, I found myself giving even more through my work as an attorney, as a volunteer in my community, and to my family and friends.

I believe that once you start giving, you will want to continue giving more and more. Any generosity you show to others will improve your own life tenfold. Don't wait for others to motivate you. Take one action step every week to help someone in need. I've heard countless stories about how at the end of a person's life, they never regret not buying more things for themselves, but they do regret that they didn't give more to help others in need.

We make a living by what we get, but we make a life by what we give.
–ATTRIBUTED TO WINSTON CHURCHILL

If you are not sure whether you have the time, resources, or inclination to give, consider that there is scientific proof that giving can make you happier, protect your health, and prolong your life. Through MRI technology, we now know that giving activates the same parts of the brain that are stimulated by food and sex. Experiments show evidence that altruism is hardwired into the brain—and it's pleasurable. In countless studies conducted around the world, it has been consistently shown that people who spend on others are happier than when they spend money on themselves. Giving can expand every aspect of life exponentially. Every day that goes by without helping another is an opportunity missed in making your life better.

In a 2017 study carried out in the Department of Economics at the University of Zurich by Soyoung Park and her colleagues, fifty people were asked to report on their levels of happiness after performing acts of generosity. The participants were given twenty-five Swiss francs (about twenty-five U.S. dollars at the time) once a week for a month, and half were asked to spend it on themselves, while the other half were instructed to choose a new person each week to spend the money on. In other words, half the volunteers agreed to be selfish and the other half to be generous. After the study, participants were asked about their mood and happiness levels, and those who had spent the money on others reported feeling significantly happier than those who spent it on themselves. Consistently, the results showed that being generous felt good.

The participants' reactions to giving were also measured using fMRI machines. A computer screen flashed hypothetical scenarios involving giving a money gift to a loved one, and the subjects' brain activity was monitored to see how they would react. The fMRI scans showed greater activity in the part of the brain associated with altruism and greater functional connectivity and communication with the brain's reward center.

Even just volunteering one's time has shown to significantly increase people's happiness. A University of Exeter study found that volunteering decreased mortality rates and improved happiness; researchers demonstrated that this was the result of increased social inclusion and activity. Across several studies, volunteers had a 22 percent lower mortality rate than non-volunteers. They were less depressed and showed more life satisfaction. Researchers at the Harvard Business School conducted studies that confirmed that happier people give more and that giving makes people happier, suggesting that happiness and giving may operate in a positive feedback loop. Others have shown that the U.S. states with the highest volunteer rates tend to also have the lowest rates of overall mortality and heart disease.

For it is in giving that we receive.
–PRAYER OF SAINT FRANCIS OF ASSISI

There are so many ways to be generous to other people. You can be kind to a stranger. You could give your time, energy, ideas, or resources to individuals or organizations. Being generous can be as simple as making eye contact when you are speaking to someone, being polite to a stranger, listening carefully to another person, or giving your time to those who are less fortunate. Give more compliments; you never know when one will make someone else's day or provide comfort to a friend in a time of need. You can truly have a positive impact on everyone you meet and do your small part to make the world a better place.

One of my favorite books from growing up is called *The Giving Tree* by Shel Silverstein. It is a quintessential feel-good story, exploring the happiness a tree received just by giving to others, and was one of my earliest introductions to the concept of giving. Although *The Giving Tree* is primarily about the complexity of human connection, it is also a story about the beauty of generosity and the power of creating a connection between two beings.

My mom and dad felt strongly about community involvement and passed this generosity down to their four children. We would always try to find ways to give to organizations and be involved with philanthropic endeavors, which allowed us to be part of our larger community and build connections that have lasted a lifetime. When asked about her experience, my mother will tell you that she is "grateful for the organizations that gave her the ability to work with them and make the community and world a better place." My mom came to the United States from Cuba as an immigrant with very little and felt strongly about giving back with her time and, eventually, philanthropy. My parents were examples to me and my three brothers on how to share your blessings with those in need. I am thankful that today my parents are still with us and able to be significant role models to their children, grandchildren, and community.

I have a bumper sticker on my car that says, "Give more than you take." This mantra has served me well in helping to create a fulfilling and happy life; I never expected that I would receive so much more in return. When going through the toughest of times, it was the people I once gave to who helped me when I needed it most. My children have had several medical issues, and there were times when I needed the support of my friends to help me find doctors, provide a shoulder to cry on, or step in to help care for my other children when I couldn't. I remember when my son had breath-holding spells; he would stop breathing for as long as a minute every time he cried and sometimes would lose consciousness. Others stepped up to cover my family and work responsibilities so I could stay by his side. I remember having deadlines at work where I needed to stay late and was able to call a family member or friend to pick up a child from school. I remember missing my daughter's dance recital because I was on a trip but knew I could rely on my husband, mom, and friend to cheer her on. I have met remarkable people and forged many wonderful relationships through my children, work, and community involvement.

Sometimes giving doesn't come naturally, so when life gets a little busy, you may have to schedule time to give back. Before my last birthday, I made a conscious decision to do one generous act a day for the fifty days leading up to the event. At times it was a struggle to make time or come up with an idea, but once I committed, I made sure I followed through with one act of kindness every day, even if it was small.

My final list, compiled with the help of friends, included the following:

- Opening the door for a stranger
- Paying for the person behind me in a drive-through
- Donating to a GoFundMe page
- Dropping food off at a homeless shelter
- Picking up litter
- Donating blankets to a shelter
- Giving an umbrella to someone stuck in the rain
- Donating dog toys to an animal shelter
- Cleaning my closet and donating clothing and shoes
- Creating and distributing blessing bags (supplies for people experiencing homelessness)
- Giving up a good parking spot
- Complimenting a stranger
- Dropping off toys at a youth center
- Visiting a sick friend
- Helping a fellow airline passenger put bags up in the overhead bin
- Mentoring a youth
- Writing a thank-you card
- Sending flowers to people in nursing homes
- Doing a favor for a friend

By sharing news about my fifty-day project, other people were inspired to do the same. When my birthday arrived, I felt a huge sense of accomplishment, fulfillment, and happiness. Imagine the joy if every person could replicate just a few of these actions on a regular basis.

Give with purpose

Some believe that if they have limited financial resources, they can't be generous. Or that they should wait until after they make all their money to give back. Don't wait—anyone can give kindness, time, or enthusiasm. Studies show that giving any kind of charity, volunteering time, and even donating blood can lead people to have fuller and happier lives.

> Giving back is as good for you as it is for those you are helping, because giving gives you purpose. When you have a purpose-driven life, you're a happier person.
>
> **–GOLDIE HAWN**

The key is to find the approach that fits you—because when you do, the more you give, the more you stand to gain purpose, meaning, and happiness. According to Jenny Santi, a philanthropy advisor and author of *The Giving Way to Happiness: Stories and Science Behind the Life-Changing Power of Giving*, these are the very things that we look for in life that are often so hard to find. I've included some of her tips below to get you started:

1. **Find your passion.** Santi believes that "passion should be the foundation for giving." It is important that you choose something that you care about. It will benefit you, the specific cause, and how you spend your time if you select something you are excited about. It becomes more organic when you are enthusiastic about your

choice. Choose what is right for you and not based on someone else's feelings.

2. **Give your time.** Additionally, Santi reiterates that "the gift of time is often more valuable to the receiver and more satisfying for the giver than the gift of money." Everyone has time to give and help others. For some, it can be a small amount of time. For others, it may be a few days a month.

3. **Find an organization that aligns their mission with your interests.** There are a wide range of nonprofit organizations serving different needs throughout the world. Find an organization that supports a cause you are passionate about. Donate, make connections, share resources or time to make a difference. It may be difficult to take the first step, so either set a time on your calendar to research an organization, sign up for an event (and bring a friend along), or reach out to a colleague or acquaintance who is involved in the organization to find out more.

4. **Combine your skills, interests, and knowledge with the needs of others.** It is important to match your skills, professional experience, abilities, and interests with the needs of others. As an attorney, I have donated my expertise by providing legal advice at pro-bono clinics, representing children who are in foster care, and drafting legal documents for nonprofit organizations. My sister-in-law, a physician, took time to volunteer as a medic in Haiti after a devastating earthquake. I know a fitness instructor who organizes exercise events to raise money for a cause close to her heart. I know accountants and bankers who volunteer with nonprofits and help with the finances. Everyone has a

skill or expertise that can be useful to an organization. Consider what your interests are and find a local organization that will help you match your strengths and abilities to a worthy cause.

5. **Be proactive, not reactive.** Make the first move and don't wait to be asked by a friend or colleague. It is important to find something you care about and volunteer in that field. Don't just wait to be asked. You can make an impact, whether it is with your time, money, resources, or connections. If you are an animal lover, you can volunteer at an animal shelter. If you are passionate about helping kids, you can mentor youth or volunteer at a school. If you are passionate about the environment, get involved with one of the many organizations helping to preserve and protect nature or combat climate change. I am passionate about giving my time to helping young girls, so I mentor with a local organization. Never hesitate to volunteer because you think that one person can't make a difference. As Dr. Seuss says, "To the world you may be one person, but to one person you may be the world."

There are so many ways to give

Philanthropy is the art of deliberate generosity, and it does not have to be extravagant. It can be as simple as helping someone carry their groceries to their car or feeding your neighbor's dog while they're away. No matter our current circumstances, we can all have a positive impact on our community and the world.

It can be hard to know where to start, so if you are unsure what to do to give back, don't be afraid to ask. Talk to someone at your child's school, sporting club, or any other local organization that you feel a connection to in some way. Let them know of your desire to help and share some ideas of what you might be able to do. Even if you are not sure exactly how you can help, there are often already good structures and processes in place within community organizations, and the people there can match your skills with a task or role that needs to be filled.

Here are a few ideas to spark your giving side and get you serving those who need help in your community:

Volunteer at a local school. Educators and administrators are often stretched and appreciate support from parents and members of the community. I have been fortunate enough to mentor at several schools throughout my city, and it is my experience that schools work best when we all get involved. I have many friends who work with their local PTAs or chaperone field trips because they know that it is everyone's responsibility to raise our children and eliminate the existing achievement gaps in our education system. On top of this, when you volunteer at your children's school, you show them that you care and are interested in their education.

Another way to help schools is to work on a beautification project in your city. I have taken my children several times to paint walls and plant trees and gardens at local schools. There are often opportunities listed in the newspaper or on organization websites and social media about certain days, like Martin Luther King Jr. Day or Presidents' Day, when you can volunteer to beautify a school. This kind of project is not only fun but a great way to show even very young children how to give back to their community.

Offer to help families in need. Every year before the holidays, the *Miami Herald* publishes a list of local families who are in need of support in various ways. For more than thirty-five years, members of the community have dug deep to donate goods, services, and money to help those in their community who need it most. Some of the wonderful examples of people who received generous assistance include a man whose home was made accessible after he was paralyzed by a carjacker; an elderly woman who received free dental surgery and implants when she couldn't afford a new set of dentures; a young child suffering from a rare genetic disease who received a laptop so she could do her homework; a veteran battling cancer who received help with clothing, food, financial assistance, and housing; a widow who fell and broke her hip who had an aluminum ramp installed to her front door; and a young woman who was the first in her family to graduate from high school and go to college who received help to purchase clothing and books for school. You don't need to wait until you hear about stories like these; you can call a local charity organization and simply ask what families need.

Visit a retirement home. I remember going to visit my mother-in-law at her retirement community nearby. During the holidays, my children would sing songs to her and her neighbors. In just a few minutes, they had the residents singing along and swaying to the music. These visits would brighten up the days of these seniors, sometimes making their entire week. Many residents are isolated from family, and conversation and connections with people mean a great deal to them. You can volunteer to help seniors complete their daily tasks, accompany them on a shopping trip, help them to use technology, or just schedule regular visits to provided much-appreciated companionship and conversation.

Help feed the hungry. As I mentioned earlier, I used to volunteer with my son at a homeless shelter on the weekends, serving food to the residents. Not only was this helpful to the shelter, it also exposed me and my son to a wonderful community. You can also donate food or money to an organization feeding the hungry or, next time you shop, buy some extra canned vegetables, pasta, or any kind of nonperishable food and drop it off at a nearby food bank. Despite America's overall prosperity, there are many who go hungry—almost 37 million Americans suffered from food insecurity in 2018.

Donate or fundraise. If you have excess household items or clothing, you can donate them to an organization that supports those in need or organize a yard sale and give the proceeds to your favorite charity. A community drive or charity event is another way to raise money or gather in-kind donations on a larger scale. Donating in this way can make an immediate difference in someone else's life, providing diapers for a new mom, canned foods for a food pantry, or furniture and appliances for a family whose home was destroyed.

Be a good neighbor. During hurricane season, my neighbors are often out helping one another to shutter houses and businesses, sharing ideas and tools. Participating in a neighborhood effort builds a sense of community and increases your connection to those around you. Volunteering your time and energy can strengthen your community, and a simple gesture of kindness to a neighbor, like helping to move a piece of furniture, can be the start of a new friendship.

Help a stranger in need. If you find an opportunity to (safely) help someone you don't know—no strings attached, just because you can—it sends a powerful message of generosity and kindness into the world. Again, this can be as simple as helping someone struggling to get their groceries to their car or opening a door for someone who has their hands full. Follow it up with a smile and you've made a positive and meaningful impression on someone's day.

Become a docent. Museums, art galleries, presidential libraries, aquariums, zoos, and universities frequently need trained guides to lead people through the facilities and enhance the visitors' experience. If you enjoy being around people, volunteering at your local museum or theater could be enjoyable and enlightening.

Volunteer at a hospital. Hospital volunteers provide crucial support to hospitals and also offer comfort and convenience to patients, families, and visitors. Volunteer opportunities include everything from manning information booths to sitting with patients or entertaining children.

Police, fire, rescue—recognize those who serve. Giving back to the community can also mean giving to those who serve or have served. Police and fire departments, local military bases, and local veterans' organizations offer the opportunity to recognize and thank those who keep our community and our nation safe. You can remember them with treats or donations at the holidays or anytime. About a year ago, I took my daughter and her friend to deliver homemade cookies to the local fire department. The firefighters felt appreciated and were delighted to receive this surprise. My daughter and her friend were happy to give back to people who risk their lives for our community and learned an important lesson.

Disaster relief. When disasters strike, communities come together to care for their own who are affected by the storm, earthquake, flood, or other catastrophe. This is an important time to get involved and give back, as the needs are immense and immediate. The donations needed will depend on the extent and type of disaster—anything from clothes and blankets to a new home or building. Form a disaster response team, if one isn't already in place, to meet these needs.

Environment. Pick up litter or plant a tree. Trees are essential not only for the environment but to us as well, especially in a time when air pollution is a growing issue. With each tree planted, we help clean the air and encourage wildlife and wellness. Recycle your plastic at a local recycling center or join or start a clean-up project at a nearby park or beach.

Pay it forward. Next time you order a coffee, pay for the person behind you. Or, when you are at the market, pay an extra few dollars toward the next person's bill. This will be appreciated and encourage the next person to pay it forward too.

Volunteer at your church, synagogue, mosque, or other religious institution. This can help your fellow members and the community at large.

Pet therapy. My friend is part of a pet therapy team. She and her dog visit people in the hospital who are lonely, hurting, and missing their own pets. She spends her time with them and their families and brings them joy. Giving this time certainly makes a difference in these people's day.

Giving at work

It has been shown that giving at work—whether by sharing an article, offering some quick feedback, giving credit for work done well, joining or creating an organization whose focus is on giving—will eventually contribute to your own success.

According to Adam Grant, author of *Give and Take: A Revolutionary Approach to Success*, givers enjoy contributing more to others than they receive in return. For example, they make introductions. They share knowledge and offer help with no strings attached. He shows data that suggest on many levels that creating value for other people is the best way for everyone to win in the long run, even though being generous in the short run may involve some costs.

"Selfless giving, in the absence of self-preservation instincts, easily becomes overwhelming," says Grant. It is important to be "otherish," which he defines as being willing to give more than you receive but still keeping your own interests in sight.

There are several ways to show generosity that can eventually bring you more success as a leader at work: appreciating the achievements of others, soliciting and considering others' opinions, and showing kindness, even when you don't agree with someone else's idea or direction.

And this is true not only at work, but also at home. People who live their lives like givers experience a greater sense of meaning because they feel their actions really matter. Giving helps build relationships that will help you through your personal or professional life.

Business leader Warren Buffett is a firm advocate for the importance of giving: "If you're in the luckiest one percent of humanity, you owe it to the rest of humanity to think about the other ninety-nine percent." And that includes giving more while you're at work.

SEVEN ACTION STEPS
TO GIVE MORE

1. Declutter your closets and cupboards and donate anything that could be of use to someone else to a local charity.

2. Find a way to donate to a good cause at least once a month—this could be your time, goods, or a cash donation, depending on your circumstances.

3. Review your skills and expertise and match them with an organization that could use some help.

4. Join forces with a friend or colleague to explore ways you can contribute to a good cause together.

5. Be on the lookout for small ways you can help others as you go about your day. Simple acts like offering a seat on a crowded bus or helping someone with a flat tire can mean a lot.

6. If you are a parent, offer to help out at your child's school or sports club.

7. Look for ways to be more helpful at work, championing and supporting your colleagues whenever you can.

THOUGHTS AND ACTIONS TOWARD GIVING MORE

When was the last time you gave a gift for no reason or performed an act of kindness?

When was the last time you volunteered your time?

What was your last donation of any amount?

Write down three action steps you will schedule on your calendar:
Some ideas include volunteering at least once a month, donating any amount to any campaign, giving a gift, and doing one act of kindness a week.

1.

2.

3.

MORE THOUGHTS

_____

_____

_____

_____

_____

_____

_____

_____

_____

_____

_____

_____

_____

GIVE MORE

_____

_____

_____

_____

_____

_____

_____

_____

_____

_____

_____

_____

_____

_____

MORE

_____

_____

_____

_____

_____

_____

_____

_____

_____

_____

_____

_____

_____

_____

CHAPTER 4

More Balance

Balance is not something you find, it is something you create.

–JANA KINGSFORD

The hardest thing to find in life is balance—especially the more success you have, the more you look to the other side of the gate. What do I need to stay grounded, in touch, in love, connected, emotionally balanced? Look within yourself.

–CELINE DION

Kate Davis is a speaker, writer, comedian, and actress who is also a mom to three kids. In her books, comedy shows, and speaking engagements, she uses humor to express creative solutions to managing frustrations and finding balance. Juggling home, life, and work commitments is not easy; she summed the situation up perfectly when she started a show by saying, "I've got to do this fast because I have three kids at home who think I'm at the store right now!"

If you are constantly trying to squeeze too much into your day, her predicament will be all too familiar. When you are juggling multiple demands, responsibilities, and commitments, life balance can seem impossible. Bringing a sense of humor to the situation certainly helps, but there are many other practical strategies you can deploy to find and maintain the balance you seek.

At each stage of life, your focus will be different. Whether you are going to school, building a career, or starting a family, there will be things you want to do and things you must do. The challenge is to find a balance that allows you the time to do what you enjoy while still fulfilling your responsibilities. It's also important to realize that balance is not perfection. It does not involve cramming your schedule chock-full of every activity imaginable. There have been many periods of my life where I struggled to find balance and felt unable to meet my responsibilities in my professional and personal life. Just like the mom in the poem "If You Give a Mom a Muffin" by Beth Brubaker and Kathy Fictorie, there were days I felt like I was running around frantically but not accomplishing anything at all. I felt burned out, like many other women. During these times, I looked for advice and tools that would help me navigate the chaos.

Balance is crucial to your health, happiness, and contentment. It allows you to grow as an individual and arrive at a place of mental peace and well-being. When you find more balance, it will positively impact so many areas of your life, including:

- **Improved health.** If you are constantly doing too much, the stress will eventually make you sick—but with an achievable to-do list you'll avoid many unnecessary health issues.
- **Better sleep.** With boundaries in place to bring balance to your daily life, you can significantly improve the quality and quantity of your sleep.
- **Less pressure.** When you remove the pressure, you will feel more content, have more energy, and deal far better with your emotions and frustrations.
- **Less stress.** If you are successfully managing your work time, your stress levels will be much lower than if you are juggling being on call or trying to catch up on work after hours.
- **More efficient.** With balance in your days, you will be better able to focus your energies, so you can be more productive and get more done.
- **More time for you.** Consistently working after hours robs you of time for yourself. With balance, you can schedule in the activities you have been looking forward to.
- **More social life.** Being perpetually busy means you'll miss so many precious moments with family and friends—with balance you can be present.

Finding your balance

When asked by someone how your day is going, do you ever answer, "Busy"? I know I do. We are constantly bombarded by multiple obligations and tasks. There are unexpected struggles and disruptions on a daily basis. In today's high-tech world, smartphones, laptops, and social media are all easily accessible 24/7, eager for our attention. The technology itself is not bad; we just need to manage it better so that we can become more productive, healthier, and happier.

A balanced life looks different to each of us. That's why it's important to assess your life as it is now, find where you could benefit from more balance, and make a conscious decision of how you will make that happen. Set concrete goals, being sure to make time for yourself on a daily basis.

Creating more balance begins with a shift in mindset, from being constantly harried to having a sense of control. Some simple actions will help: setting your priorities, tracking your time, concentrating on one task or person at a time, assessing your habits, and setting boundaries between your personal and professional life.

Sadly, for many, multitasking still reigns supreme. Distractions constantly sabotage us. Being aware of the issue and setting boundaries are key to removing distractions and achieving better results.

On the brink of burnout

Rachel Montañez wrote an article for *Forbes* about navigating career changes, career paths, burnout, and work-life balance. She discussed how we're not as productive as we could be and predicted that we are headed toward a burnout epidemic. While most top companies now offer parental leave and flexible work patterns, most people still struggle to achieve a healthy balance.

Software company RescueTime conducted a study in 2019 that analyzed 185 million work hours. They found that 21 percent of those hours are spent on social media, entertainment, and news; and 40 percent of our day is spent "multitasking with communication tools." We also check email and instant messaging every six minutes! This multitasking distracts us and significantly reduces our productivity.

With more time spent on our devices than ever before, we have less time to get work done during normal business hours—which means we end up working earlier, later, and on weekends. It is thought that up to a third of salaried workers are working on the weekend. The RescueTime study estimated that people do around a quarter of their work outside regular business hours, with 28 percent starting their day before eight thirty in the morning and 40 percent using their computers after ten at night, significantly reducing sleep quality.

According to a Harvard Business School survey, 94 percent of professionals in the service industry put in more than fifty hours a week. On average, Americans now work more than forty-seven hours a week, one of the highest totals in the world. And while some may claim they have no option but to put in the hours to get the job done, it comes at a cost; when work and life are unbalanced, it has a negative impact on our health, well-being, and relationships. Finding time and space to rest and regenerate is a must if we want to avoid the very real possibility of burnout.

Being aware of how you are working and understanding the values that support work-life balance are key to addressing the problem. Having the power to fit your work life in your pocket with a smartphone, the rise of the "always on" work culture, the distractions that hurt our productivity, and our inability to use our time wisely is unbalancing us all. It is negatively impacting our sleep, health, relationships, productivity, and happiness. It's no wonder so many people are struggling.

I think about the many times I worked in bed at night, with my laptop on well beyond ten o'clock. This has impacted my stress and happiness levels, which in turn impacts my ability to be my best at work and as a mother, wife, and friend. When I am off-balance, I have a harder time communicating, collaborating, and getting things done. Even as I sit here and write this book, I am aware of the many distractions that surround me, threatening my productivity and the balance I am working to achieve. What helps me is to put my phone on the other side of the room and close my door. I also allot a certain amount of time to writing and try to stick to those parameters. Workplace distractions, wasting time, and simply being inefficient with the time we do have, all increase the likelihood that we'll lose balance and end up working outside of work hours.

How to get your life back into balance

These days everyone is really busy. We juggle responsibilities relating to family, work, activities, and community. So how do we prioritize what really matters? How do we prioritize self-care? How do we eliminate distractions? How do we achieve more in our day?

When your life is unbalanced, it feels like you have no choices. Your purpose, values, and priorities are neglected. Instead of living your life the way you want, you are constantly pulled in other directions.

Do you feel like your to-do list is never-ending? Do you feel you are very busy but not sure you are accomplishing anything? Do you feel like you are living on someone else's schedule and have lost your direction? If the answer is yes, it is time to take charge—otherwise the likely result will be frustration, stress, and exhaustion.

Jory MacKay, editor of the RescueTime blog, has written about work-life balance and how it is under attack. He recommends ways you can protect it, such as blocking certain websites for set periods of time so you can be more productive. If you find it difficult to focus and avoid distractions while working, there are plenty of apps and websites that can support you in achieving more with your time. By setting proper boundaries and eliminating distractions, multitasking, and work overload, you'll free up more of your time and will be a step closer to finding some balance.

Realistically, we all know there is no such thing as perfect balance, but there are strategies we can use to improve how we spend our days and get to a point where we feel calm and in control. Here are some simple but powerful actions you can take today to introduce more balance into your life:

- Realize and accept that you can't do everything at the same time. Admit where in your life you are lacking balance.
- List your priorities, values, and goals, and make sure that your tasks are aligned with them. At a recent conference I attended, we had to pick our top six values and try to align them with our daily activities. It was not easy, but I found it very valuable in shifting my mindset about what was most important. The values I picked were loyalty, personal growth, collaboration, social responsibility, integrity, and family. These values may change over time, so it is important to do this exercise again every year or two to make sure you are spending time in a way that aligns with your values.
- Identify what you want to accomplish in a certain day, week, or month and who you want to spend your time

with. Every Sunday afternoon, I look at my calendar and to-do list and plan what to accomplish that week and how I'm going to do it.

- Choose people who are supportive and make your happy. These are the people who you should be making plans to see in your free time.

- Manage your schedule. Analyze what you can accomplish in twenty-four hours. We have the power to manage our time and choose how to fill it. Don't add extra tasks in a day if you know there is no time for them. Also acknowledge when you don't have control over a certain event in your calendar.

- Eliminate activities that don't fulfill any of your priorities. Pick which activities you are willing to take off your list in order to make room for more fulfilling and productive ones.

- For the activities you do keep on your list, determine which are less important or can wait and schedule them for a later date. This will instantly make you feel less stressed and overwhelmed.

- Learn how to say NO. This is something I have always struggled with, and it has taken me a long time to achieve, especially with certain events and tasks. To be honest, it is still a weakness of mine that needs to be improved. Saying no to a project, person, or organization can be difficult but necessary. When someone asks you to do something, take a pause before you say yes. Determine if you have the time and whether it fits with your list of priorities and values. If you are not sure what to do, don't give an immediate answer; let them know you need time to think.

- Schedule time for yourself—literally schedule time in your calendar to do the things you enjoy like exercising, talking with an old friend, reading, or taking a walk. Is there a hobby that you have always wanted to take up? Is there a volunteer opportunity that has been on your list for years? Make time for things that fulfill you. It takes deliberate effort on your part to make it happen. My friend recently told me that carving out some time for herself in the last few years has made her happier and more productive. She felt that when her children were younger, she did not make that time for herself. She is grateful for this lesson and feels she has become more optimistic and has had a more positive impact on her family and in her community.

One way to assess how to improve the balance in your life is by tracking your time for one week. See how much time you spend doing things you don't want to do or that don't align with your priorities. You can then work toward delegating them to other people or, if possible, eliminating them from your life altogether.

It's an ongoing challenge

Your idea of what constitutes a balanced life will change over time, so you will have to reevaluate your plans periodically. Set aside time to reflect on the many facets of your life and discuss its ever-changing variables with a friend, family member, or colleague. If possible, find a mentor who can give you advice on setting priorities and managing your time and offer guidance on how to say no when something doesn't align with your values.

Once you find a balance that works for the current moment in your personal and professional life, you can perform optimally in both areas. But remember, you can't achieve anything if you're unhealthy, so make sure you get plenty of exercise, eat properly, and sleep well. Your health should come first. While you may be able to function adequately and get away with burning the candle at both ends for a while (especially when you're young), at some point it will catch up with you, and burnout is a real possibility.

It also pays to be organized. Set aside time at the start of the week to plan your schedule. Include appointments and work commitments, as well as time for yourself and your family. Recreation time is a must, even when you're busy, as it will recharge your batteries and make you more efficient in the long run. Ideally, plan to spend some time each day doing something you enjoy, to relax and recharge—walking, exercising, listening to music, reading, meditating, or having a soak in the bath.

While planning is essential, you should also be prepared to be flexible. There will always be unexpected situations that will throw your schedule out. Rather than get stressed and upset, learn to keep things in perspective and try to make the best of it when something happens that is out of your control. It is fine to experience some level of burnout; everyone does at some point. What is important is to accept it, not beat yourself up about it, learn from any mistakes you have made, and move forward. Life is never smooth sailing, and when you can learn to deal with the unexpected with calmness and a positive attitude, you will minimize the impact it has and bounce back faster.

Putting it into practice

If you struggle with finding balance, it can seem like achieving it is impossible. But if you work hard to find the right mix of your opportunities, your passions, and your talents, you can achieve it. Of course, what balance looks like is different for everyone; a life that feels balanced and attainable to one person may not be to another.

Managing your time in a more balanced and productive way leads to less stress, more peace, more accomplishment, more time to enjoy and celebrate life, and more happiness. One key to successful time management described by Stephen Covey, author of *The 7 Habits of Highly Effective People,* is learning to distinguish between what is urgent and what is important. Urgent tasks put us in a reactive mode, where we tend to be defensive, negative, hurried, and narrowly focused. Important tasks are things that contribute to our long-term mission, values, and goals. A common mistake for many is to constantly prioritize urgent tasks over important ones. This is problematic, as important (but not urgent) tasks often represent the actions and strategies necessary for you to improve and grow. Be sure to manage your time so both kinds of tasks are addressed. You may find you have to schedule the important tasks so they are not ignored.

Managing your time better and prioritizing your tasks will cut down on your feelings of busyness and allow you to work on your long-term goals. *Inc.* magazine notes that management expert Peter Drucker has said that "effective leaders manage and consolidate their time. If you hold yourself fully accountable for how you spend your time, you can make conscious choices to limit your busyness and focus on top priorities." Warren Buffett famously has a nearly empty calendar, which gives him flexibility to spend time thinking and strategizing rather than sitting in meetings all day. In her book *168 Hours*, author Laura Vanderkam put forward an interesting strategy toward life balance. She had women track their time for all 168 hours of their week. When she looked at their journals, she realized that they were overestimating the time they spent at work and doing household chores—there really was time for them to do the things they wanted if they managed their time better. With her help, the women came up with time management strategies—including keeping a time log, moving work around, building in space to focus on tasks and relationships, getting as much help as they need, inserting schedule buffers, saying no, and staying disciplined—that would let them find time for what was important to them.

When it comes to sticking to new habits, accountability and reward systems can be helpful. Getting an accountability partner (a friend, colleague, or family member who will help you prioritize your goals and check in with you regularly to discuss your situation) and rewarding yourself at the end of the week if habits change can be great ways to make your life more balanced. Daniel Pink writes in his book *When: The Scientific Secrets of Perfect Timing* that *when* you do things can have a big impact on how well you do them. In fact, time of day explains about 20 percent of the variance in human performance on cognitive tasks. Doing the right work at the right time can produce dramatically better results.

Another useful strategy is to break down larger goals into smaller, more manageable pieces and then organize them according to your priorities. Ranking in some way is necessary because it's unlikely you will ever have enough time to do everything on your list. Try not to be complicated—be decisive, keep it simple, set boundaries, know when to say no, be easy on yourself, and know that it's OK to take breaks.

Early in my career as an attorney, I remember being in a meeting and telling another attorney that I didn't have enough time to do something. I remember being called out and realized that I needed to prioritize things differently. At the time, I was juggling work and young kids, and I recognized what the problem was: I could not say no. It took me years to accept that I needed to say no to get more balance and more productivity in my life. I could have it all; I just couldn't have it all at the same time. I needed to learn how to prioritize.

I also got better at scheduling time, not just for work and my kids, but time that I needed for myself, whether it was running or spending an evening with my husband or friends. When bad things happen to a friend or a family member, it always seems possible to drop everything and be there in their time of need. Why can't we make these people priorities during the good times as well?

Be strategic about how you spend your time. When a project idea or invitation comes to your attention, decide if, why, and how you want to proceed. Learn how to say no to things when you know you won't be able to finish the tasks that are necessary to accomplish it.

Thomas Davies, the director of Google for Work, focuses while at the office by designing his time, rather than managing it. He puts all his tasks into a chart divided into the following four quadrants:

- People tasks (managing teams, coaching and mentoring, etc.)
- Business development tasks (data analysis, running sales meetings, etc.)
- Transactional tasks (emails, reviewing documents, etc.)

- Representative tasks (meeting with customers, speaking at conferences, etc.)

By using the chart, he can see what areas he's spending his time on and make sure he works on the most important tasks, as well as those he enjoys, as a priority. This is how Davies labeled his quadrants, but you can label your four however you like. Managing your tasks in this way will give you a clearer idea of what you spend your time on and will show you where you're unbalanced. According to Davies, it will allow you to "design what you do, rather than just do what you need to do." You can design your time by making your own quadrants that apply to your life, sorting your tasks, and working through them based on those that are important and enjoyable.

There are lots of beneficial methods that can help you manage your tasks, including the Pomodoro Technique, where you focus yourself for set blocks of time. Some useful tools for getting organized include the Full Focus Planner by Michael Hyatt and the BestSelf Self Planner and Self Journal. There are also apps like Microsoft's To Do and Done that may be helpful. These are just a small selection—there are a multitude of other planners, strategies, and apps that can let you sharpen your focus and manage your time and priorities more effectively.

Managing your time is not easy—but when you do it well, you will have more time for the things that matter. As I mentioned earlier, I have used exercises to help me prioritize my values and consider the relevance of a new project to them before acceptance. Only you can control your time. Find a strategy that works for you—it could be making lists, planning in advance, prioritizing on your calendar, or a combination of these. As a starting point, create a values chart to help you understand and rank what's important to you. When considering adding an activity, check whether the action aligns with your values chart and how it impacts your existing priorities. And most importantly, know when to ask for help and lean on your support system when you need them.

By multitasking or juggling too many things, you will only end up splitting your focus, which lowers the quality of your work. Limit the amount of time you spend on social media by allocating an appropriate amount of time and sticking to it. Take regular breaks and make sure you rest when you need to. Avoid going over things more than once—for example, when you read an email or get a text from a colleague, reply immediately if you can. Putting it aside to handle later just means you have to turn your attention to the same task twice. These are all small things, but when practiced regularly and consistently, they will help you train your brain, form new habits, and become more balanced.

SEVEN ACTION STEPS
TO CREATE MORE BALANCE

1. Spend time every Sunday planning your schedule for the upcoming week. Include both work commitments and personal time, making sure that you don't overcommit.

2. When making your weekly plan, always schedule in time for YOU. This can be time spent doing any activity that you enjoy, whether it is exercise, meditation, organizing, or reading—whatever brings you balance.

3. At home, keep your work and personal life separate. Don't leave your work folders in your kitchen. Designate an area where you can keep them, preferably out of sight.

4. Review your mobile devices and analyze how you are spending your time on them. If needed, adjust accordingly, setting boundaries to build better digital habits.

5. Research the many tools out there designed to help you get organized, and try one that resonates with you. There are lots of useful apps, websites, journals, and coaches that can really make a difference.

6. Don't try to do it all and don't say yes to everything. The ability to balance your life as much as you can will bring you more joy and contentment.

7. Avoid multitasking, both at home and at work. You'll always get more done and to a higher standard when you can stay focused on the task at hand.

THOUGHTS AND ACTIONS TOWARD MORE BALANCE

Do you feel like you have balance in your life?

In which parts of your life would you like to see more balance?

What are your priorities?

Write down three action steps you will schedule on your calendar:
Some ideas include examining and prioritizing tasks, asking for help, setting boundaries, and creating a values chart.

1.

2.

3.

MORE THOUGHTS

MORE BALANCE

MORE

CHAPTER 5

Connect More

The healing of our present roundedness may lie in recognizing and reclaiming the capacity we all have to heal each other, the enormous power in the simplest of human relationships: the strength of a touch, the blessing of forgiveness, the grace of someone else taking you just as you are and finding in you an unsuspected goodness.

–RACHEL NAOMI REMEN

Eddie Jaku experienced hell during the Holocaust, yet he thinks of himself as "the happiest man on earth." In 2019, at ninety-nine years of age, he beautifully described the importance of friendship during a TED Talk:

I wonder how people exist without friendship, without people to share their secrets, hopes, and dreams, to share good fortune or sad losses. In the sweetness of friendship, let there be laughter and sharing of pleasure, good times made better and bad times forgotten—due to the magic of friendship.

Over time, I have grown to understand the importance of relationships and can appreciate the impact they have had on each stage of my life. Strong relationships can bring you happiness, health, deeper meaning, and even longevity. Friends and family you are close with can offer support and advice during desperate and lonely times and can make an enormous difference in your world. People enter your life for different reasons. Even negative people play a role, helping you to identify what you need (and don't need) in a friend and build resilience to toxic situations. I have spent many hours discussing this topic with my children. At one point, they have each felt disappointed, hurt, or left out by friends. I try to convey to them the message that took me years to really understand: that every interaction, even the negative ones, will serve a purpose.

Social connections are pivotal, in both your community and work environments. Research highlights their many benefits, from increased immunity to lower rates of anxiety and depression. "Humans need others to survive," says psychologist Julianne Holt-Lunstad of Brigham Young University. "Regardless of one's sex, country, or culture of origin, or age or economic background, social connection is crucial to human development, health, and survival."

In 2010, Holt-Lunstad published research showing that people who had weaker social ties had a 50 percent increased likelihood of premature death than those with stronger ties. Being disconnected socially, she showed, posed danger comparable to smoking fifteen cigarettes a day and was more predictive of early death than the effects of air pollution and physical inactivity.

John Cacioppo pioneered the field of social neuroscience and dedicated more than two decades to studying loneliness. His findings show how misunderstood the concept has been. Traditionally and incorrectly associated with social isolation, depression, introversion, and poor social skills, loneliness in fact "is a unique condition in which an individual perceives himself or herself to be socially isolated even when among other people. . . . The deleterious effects of loneliness are not attributable to some peculiarity of individuals who are lonely, instead they are due to the effects of loneliness on ordinary people." Loneliness does not discriminate by socioeconomic status, ethnicity, or gender. It can affect anyone. You can have what is perceived by the world as "everything"—a hundred friends, a fascinating career—and still feel lonely.

Because of social media platforms such as Facebook, Twitter, Snapchat, and Instagram, many of us remain in contact with our high school friends and former co-workers—but in our daily lives, our communities are shrinking. We create two kinds of connection—strong ties are those that exist between close friends and family members who interact frequently. Weak ties involve less interaction, making people more like acquaintances. The ties made through social media can be valuable but are considered weak ties. Strong ties are the ones that are important for our stability, contentment, and ability to develop robust connections and communities. Between 1985 and 2009, the average size of social networks in America declined by more than one-third. We may have hundreds of friends on social media, but evidence is growing that those connections are not the ones that provide us with what we need: human contact. Instead, the more virtually connected we become, the more we seem to let our face-to-face relationships decline. Whether it is catching up with an old friend or inviting a neighbor over for coffee, talking with someone in your vanpool on the way to work or getting coffee from a café where you know the barista's name, these are the interactions that feed our social needs.

A few years ago, I bought a cell phone jail with its own lock and key that I keep in my kitchen. Each family member puts their phone in the cell block during meals and family meetings. If not, we would all at some point check our messages or social media. At restaurants, everyone has to put their phone facedown and in the middle of the table. Not only does this allow us to focus on one another, but it helps to build patience. One of my favorite cartoons shows a young couple staring at their phones at a restaurant and commenting about an elderly couple nearby, "I hope that when we're old, we don't sit at a restaurant not texting." Funny but true. While it's tempting to check and recheck your emails and news feed, we need to put down our phones more, silence our gadgets, and have real conversations. That is how we form the relationships that sustain us and make us fulfilled and happy. When you do put away your tech to connect with someone, be sure to really pay attention, listen, make eye contact, and show interest. Ask questions and look for common ground and similar values and interests. This can make all the difference in creating long-lasting and meaningful relationships that will positively impact every aspect of your life, including your health, success, happiness, and productivity.

Friendship and happiness

Friendships really matter. With good friends, we feel connected, understood, and loved for who we are. I always enjoy reading and giving greeting cards that celebrate friendships; often there are quotes or sayings inside that describe the connection beautifully. Here are a few of my favorites—I hope some remind you of the kind of relationship and fun times you enjoy with your closest friends.

- "We'll be friends until we're old and senile . . . then, we'll be new friends!" *Unknown*
- "This is by far your worst idea ever . . . I'll be there in fifteen minutes." *Unknown*
- "We've been friends for so long I can't remember which one of us is the bad influence." *Unknown*
- "It is one of the blessings of old friends that you can afford to be stupid with them." *Ralph Waldo Emerson*
- "I don't like to commit myself about heaven and hell— you see, I have friends in both places." *Mark Twain*
- "Friends are people who know you really well and like you anyway." *Greg Tamblyn*
- "A best friend is like a four-leaf clover, hard to find, lucky to have." *Unknown*
- "Friends don't let friends do stupid things . . . alone." *Unknown*
- "I don't know what's tighter, our jeans or our friendship." *Unknown*
- "There is nothing better than a friend, unless it is a friend with chocolate." *Linda Grayson*
- "We'll be best friends forever because you already know too much." *Unknown*

In a 2019 article in *Success* magazine, Harvard-trained happiness researcher and author Shawn Achor suggests that, when it comes to your friends, a mix of three types of positive influencers in your life is optimal for happiness. Here's his list:

1. **Pillars.** These are the people who are your rock in tough times. They have your back regardless: The best friend who will drop everything to come over late at night bearing ice cream, the mentor at work who will champion you for the promotion or big account, the teammate who will pick up your slack when you are overextended. You need these sources of unconditional support and acceptance.
2. **Bridges.** Additionally, you need these connectors to new people or resources outside your existing ecosystem. A bridge might be the person to invite you into a club or committee, or they might introduce you to investors who could be interested in funding your project. You'll know someone is a bridge if their connections and resources don't overlap entirely with your own. A bridge doesn't necessarily have to be of higher status to connect you with other high-potential people or big opportunities.
3. **Extenders.** We all need these positive influencers who will push us outside our comfort zones. This could be a mentor or a friend with a different skill set or different personality from your own.

Achor points out that "capitalizing on diversity requires embracing people's differences." It is important to "analyze your social circle [and] look for people who complement your tendencies and traits, and who will encourage you to cultivate positive new ones."

A study conducted by scientists at Yale looked at how our happiness and the happiness of our social networks are closely connected. Nikolas Christakis and James Fowler researched social networks and their impact on happiness. They found that social networks have clusters of happy and unhappy people, and a person's happiness extends to three degrees of separation, meaning it can influence and be influenced by their friends, their friends' friends, and the friends of people who are friends of their friends. They also discovered that people who are surrounded by many happy people are more likely to become happy in the future, and each additional happy friend increases your chances of happiness by about 9 percent.

Another study conducted by Julia Rohrer, a PhD candidate at the Max Planck Institute, focused on a large group of Germans who were committed to becoming happier. Some of the participants pursued self-improvement goals such as getting a new job or finding financial success, while the others spent more time with family and friends. A year later, Rohrer found that those who focused on connecting more with others were happier than those who pursued self-improvement. In her article in *Psychological Science* she stated, "Our results demonstrate that not all pursuits of happiness are equally successful and corroborate the great importance of social relationships for human well-being."

How to make and keep friends

I am proud of my ability to get along with and befriend various types of people from all parts of my life. I am open to connecting with others, regardless of their status or background, and I realize how important it is to talk to strangers and really listen. At times, I have been shy, but when I push myself out of my comfort zone, I am pleasantly surprised by the relationships I have formed and the knowledge I have gained. Making friends is about the connection, not about impressing people and thinking you are either too good or not good enough for them.

Smile when you meet someone new and listen to what they have to share, asking questions to identify common interests. Try to find out more about them by asking about their work, hobbies, and the people who are important to them. People like to talk about themselves and share stories. What I have also learned about people, especially when you are getting to know them, is that everyone, including myself, has a small void or insecurity. If you sense that in someone, you can always try to help them fill that void. You will create an authentic human connection, make a friend, and support another person.

This is about one human being helping another human being, and that's how friendship grows. Everyone thinks that people want to be friends with the person who's the coolest or the richest or the most accomplished. When you get right down to it, people should spend time with people who make them feel good—and that's it.

There is a saying, "To have good friends, you need to be a good friend." Make sure that you are thoughtful and caring. Ask a lot of questions to show that you are really invested. Don't just ask generic questions about their day, or how work was, or how they are—make sure you ask specific questions that show you're really thinking about them. For example, if you know that your friend had an exam yesterday, you might want to ask, "How did your test go?" and explore the experience with them. Show that you're really paying attention. And as you're asking questions, be an active listener.

To attract kind, loyal, and caring people, it is important to focus on treating people the way you would like to be treated. In *Option B,* Sheryl Sandberg and Adam Grant call this the Golden Rule, but they also discuss a higher standard—the Platinum Rule, where you treat others as they want to be treated, especially when they are suffering. They recommend that you "take a cue from the person in distress and respond with understanding—or better yet, action." Building successful relationships takes this kind of commitment. I try to improve my relationships by being a good friend, family member, and colleague, and by living up to these ideals:

1. **Be dependable.** Your friends should be able to count on you, no matter what. When you say you are going to do something or be somewhere, make it happen. If you can't be there at a particular moment, be truthful and communicate clearly. Keep your promises and avoid complicated situations.

2. **Be honest.** If you are able to open up to others and be vulnerable, they will feel comfortable and be more likely to share their lives with you. Speak your truth, even if you disagree with a friend.

3. **Be respectful.** I have friends with whom I disagree about political or social issues. Over time, I have learned to accept and respect other opinions and choices. If I am sharing my point of view, I am careful and thoughtful with my words. I also avoid conversations that could get intense and uncomfortable.

4. **Keep things confidential.** If a friend tells you private information, don't repeat it to others. Your friends should have the comfort of knowing that you will not reveal their secrets. Trust is essential for long-lasting friendships.

5. **Say sorry and learn to forgive.** When you've made a mistake, own up to it and apologize. Don't ignore it and pretend that nothing is wrong. You should also be able to forgive your friend if they are sincere and haven't done something too horrible. Recognize that nobody is perfect. What I have found over the years is that forgiveness has helped me more than it helped the person who committed the transgression. It doesn't mean I forget and am not aware of what could happen in the future, but it allows me to move past it.

6. **Be loyal.** Don't talk about your friends behind their backs and stand up for them when appropriate. I try not to say something about a friend that I would not say to their face. Avoid gossip and give the benefit of the doubt to a friend when you hear anything negative about them. Give friends the opportunity to explain themselves.

7. **Be inclusive.** Never put your friends in a position where they feel left out. Whenever I organize a gathering, I try to invite as many friends as possible, especially anyone who might feel bad if they were not included.

8. **Listen to your friends.** In conversations with others, do you end up talking about yourself, your achievements and feelings? Of course there is always room to share, but make sure you are listening, understanding, and supporting your friends when you are with them. Be a good listener and don't monopolize conversations. Listening shows that your care.

9. **Be accepting and nonjudgmental.** Accept the choices your friends make even if you don't agree with them; try to put yourself in their shoes. Don't try to change your friend. Accept them for who they are, appreciate

and celebrate your differences, and recognize that you are fortunate to be introduced to different perspectives. Expect the same from your friends. They should appreciate you and your unique personality and opinions.

10. **Be there!** Be the friend who everyone knows they can count on during the best and worst of times. When your friend gets a promotion, take them out for a meal. If your friend is sick or going through a difficult time, reach out and ask them what they need. Always be there, no matter what.

Real and meaningful friendship must always be a two-way street. We need to give as much as (or even more than) we receive. That's why, when you talk to a therapist, it doesn't feel like a satisfying connection. Because no matter how much they help us, if we are not giving aid in return, it doesn't create that mutual sense of connection.

Celebrating friendship

There are lots of ways to create fun times and good memories with your friends. Birthdays and other special occasions provide the perfect backdrop for a get-together, whether you organize a casual, inexpensive birthday celebration at home with a potluck meal or a big birthday bash where you go away together or out on the town. This is why I celebrated my recent milestone birthday with my friends at a camp in North Carolina. Coming together in this environment was memorable, casual, and fun.

Of course, you don't need to wait for a special occasion to catch up. Host a gathering for your dearest friends—for no reason at all, or as a way to say thank you for all they've done.

Sharing is another way to strengthen your bond—and this goes for the things you own as well as your talents. Don't be stingy with your possessions; always share them with your friends. And if you have a special skill or talent that could benefit them, be sure to offer it. Maybe you are a whiz at scrapbooking. Or money management. Or résumé writing. Whatever it is, share what you have generously.

Friends are always ready to celebrate each other's success. They're really happy when you get a promotion at work, start a relationship, or buy a shiny new car. Be the first to call your friend and say, "Hey, well done. Congratulations! Let's go out and celebrate." Be proud and share in their achievements.

Unfortunately, as the years pass, people tend to grow apart, especially if a friend moves away or enters a different stage of life. It may not be possible to keep every friendship because of such obstacles. If there are friendships that really matter to you, make the effort to keep in touch. I have certain friendships that have survived long distances and long periods of time. You can stay connected by setting up regular calls or sending updates. I have monthly Zoom calls with my high school friends, and this lets us keep in touch and support one another through the good and bad times. If you have local friends you haven't seen in a while, organize a lunch or fun night out. It may seem strange to schedule what used to be casual interactions, but these are some of the most important meetings you will have. If you haven't spoken to a friend in a while, schedule a time to chat. Text them that you are thinking about them. If your friendship is important to you, make the effort to maintain it.

Every friendship will evolve; people grow up, move to different places, start new jobs or a new family. Although a friendship may become different, it doesn't mean that it can't thrive and be important to you. It is normal for a relationship to take different roles in your life over the years. Appreciate the changes your friendship has made and learn to grow along with it.

How to know when friends are toxic or negative

I often remind my kids of the research I referred to in chapter 1 that says you become like the ten people you are closest to—and that they should be cautious about who their closest friends are and make sure that their values are aligned.

Take the time right now to write down the names of the ten people you spend most of your time with. Do they help you be a better and happier person? Do they get excited about your achievements? Or do they judge you, criticize you, and point out your shortcomings in an unhelpful way? If you feel that anyone you spend time with is displaying jealous, controlling, or disrespectful behavior toward you, it could be time to set physical and emotional boundaries.

If you are unable for some reason to separate from the negative people in your life, make sure you engage in healthy coping skills, stay true to your values, and realize that only you have control of yourself—no one else. I often tell my children when they have arguments with friends that the only thing they can control is their reaction. I advise them to pick their fights wisely and to realize that they don't always have to be right. Compromising instead of continuing to fight usually leads to less stress and more respect.

Making the effort to connect

Friendships shape our lives. They impact who you become and what you do, both personally and professionally. Even at work, your success and contentment depend on the support of your colleagues. People are happier at their jobs when they're in a caring and productive environment.

Creating meaningful connections takes effort, but the rewards are worth it. Each day, look for opportunities to form and build real, lasting, and satisfying relationships. Help others work toward their goals or celebrate their accomplishments and milestones. Be the one who consistently makes plans to get together or introduces others to opportunities and meaningful relationships. Each day holds so many chances to demonstrate that you care for and value the people close to you.

Even when life gets busy and you have limited time, it's important to maintain these relationships. Today, it's easy to make a call or send a text or organize a group call just to be in touch with others. If you want to expand your circle of friends and you are not sure where to start, get involved in an organization that you are passionate about or reach out to some old friends. Relying on social media is just not enough—you need to have authentic, face-to-face conversations.

I consider myself lucky that I've been able to maintain relationships from my childhood and beyond. But as I get older, I realize more clearly how important it is to put effort into every relationship, to show gratitude, be inclusive, and be present with your friends when you are with them.

It is not always easy and convenient to be a good friend, but it's worth taking the time to maintain and strengthen your relationships. Humans are social animals, and we need friends to interact with and spend time with throughout our lives.

Reliable and enjoyable friends can provide us with support and happiness; relationships based on social media exchanges are just not the same. Try to engage in at least one or two face-to-face interactions a week that will build an existing or new relationship. There is always something you can do to show that you are vested in a friendship. It costs nothing to be a good friend. The best gifts are often not material and come from the heart. Improving all our social connections and relationships is good for overall happiness, resilience, and health. Good relationships provide you support, stability and contentment. Friendship is important because as humans, we are social animals and need friends to interact with and spend time with throughout our life. Improving your social connections and friendships will increase your overall happiness and make for a more contented life.

I have come to understand that community is about a series of small choices and everyday actions, about having authentic conversations, about building a support system one relationship at a time. It's how you spend your energy and invest in other people during the good times and the bad. While our kids were growing up, little did my husband and I realize that the hours we spent at parties, birthday celebrations, sports practice, and school events were hours spent forming a community and building lifelong relationships. We also became friends with many of the people we met through the professional and nonprofit organizations we were involved with over the years.

We made friends a priority for ourselves and for our children, and it showed during our most difficult times. When my mother-in-law passed away a few years ago, our family really experienced the strength of the community we had created. My husband is an only child, so the importance of these relationships was even more apparent during this difficult time. Neighbors and friends came by and brought us food and well wishes; groups of people from school, work, community organizations, and other parts of our lives materialized to comfort my husband as he mourned the loss of his second parent and became an orphan. The events of that week and the weeks that followed demonstrated the incredible level of support available when you are part of a strong community, when you've taken the time to connect more and build a web of real friendships.

We have to make the effort in relationships for them to thrive and last. Take responsibility for building real relationships in your life, whether it's one relationship or a hundred. Pick friends that you have things in common with. Look at their values. How do they measure success? What motivates them? And do you get a sense of loyalty from them? These are things to look for when spending time with friends. These are the things to look for when you want to connect more.

SEVEN ACTION STEPS
TO CREATE MORE CONNECTION

1. Reach out to three friends, family members, or colleagues a week. Schedule it in your calendar.

2. Make plans to meet up with someone face-to-face at least once a week.

3. Don't wait for a friend to call you—be the one who reaches out.

4. Be the first to congratulate your friends on special occasions or when something good happens.

5. At least once a week, consider who might be going through a difficult time and reach out to them.

6. Be responsive to friends. If you can't speak to them at a particular moment, commit to a time when you can.

7. Identify the special friendships in your life and make the effort to maintain them, even as they grow and change.

THOUGHTS AND ACTIONS TOWARD CONNECTING MORE

Who are your ten favorite people?

Are there toxic people in your life?

When was the last time you invited some friends over to your home?

Write down three action steps you will schedule on your calendar:
Some ideas include listing birthdays and your friends' and family's other special days on your calendar and reaching out to them on those dates, checking on at least one friend a week who is going through a hard time, and following up with friends, family members, and colleagues who need help.

1.

2.

3.

MORE THOUGHTS

MORE

_____

_____

_____

_____

_____

_____

_____

_____

_____

_____

_____

_____

_____

_____

_____

CHAPTER 6

More Calm

Calm is the magic elixir that brings you to a place
of balance, harmony, and peace.

–DONALD ALTMAN

It's all about finding the calm in the chaos.

–DONNA KARAN

There is a poster in my kitchen that reads, "Keep Calm and
Carry On." This slogan was created by the British government
in 1939 and placed on motivational posters to raise the morale
of the British public during World War II. Since that time, the
well-known phrase has been used countless times to inspire
people to persist through a challenge. In the midst of work,
family, and modern-day chaos, sometimes I just need to take

a look at this poster to channel my inner calm, reduce stress, and lower my anxiety.

I have seen many variations on my poster, including:

- Keep Calm and Hug Your Dog
- Keep Calm and Start Over Tomorrow
- Keep Calm and Eat Cake
- Keep Calm and Laugh with Friends
- Keep Calm and Watch a Disney Movie
- Keep Calm and Call a Psychologist
- Keep Calm and Drink Tea
- Keep Calm and Go Shopping
- Keep Calm and Sparkle
- Keep Calm and Just Do It
- Keep Calm and Write On
- Keep Calm and Nope . . . Just Lost It

The proliferation of these posters (and coffee mugs and key chains and so on) speaks to a yearning for calm in our fast-paced world, where people are juggling careers, hobbies, commitments, friends, and family. How is it possible to maintain a peaceful existence? How does anyone keep calm and lower their stress?

Most people underestimate the importance of remaining calm. It allows you to accomplish more, stay healthier, overcome your biggest fears, and find strength during the most difficult times. When you are calm, you have a much greater chance of overcoming obstacles and creating your own solutions for problems large and small.

Until recently, I found it difficult to stay calm in stressful situations, but I now use a range of tools I have developed that really help. I know that sometimes the only solution is to walk away and keep silent; this is when I need to reflect before taking action. There are times when it is better to stay quiet and calm instead of crying out. I know from personal experience that keeping calm is not easy, but we all need to keep trying—because when you can stay calm, no matter what the situation, you are better equipped to resolve disputes, avoid unhealthy and depressed feelings, and move forward with a positive attitude.

Why calm matters

Calm is a state of bliss most of us don't achieve. When you keep calm, even in the most challenging situations, you open up the avenues for solutions. This can allow you to deal better with everything from small daily annoyances to major life-changing crises.

The benefits of keeping calm include better health. According to the Johns Hopkins Medicine website, "People who feel angry often and fail to deal with it well are more likely to have heart problems, including heart attack." In a separate study published in *European Heart Journal* in 2014, the incidence of heart attack was almost five times higher in the two hours after an angry outburst, and the risk of stroke increased three-fold. The study also showed that the more intense or frequent the blowups, the higher one's heart risks.

Staying calm also allows you to communicate and think more clearly. Clarity of mind is extremely important while you are dealing with problems. In my profession as an attorney and mediator, I have witnessed countless times that when people remain calm, they are able to discuss and resolve issues in a more timely and reasonable manner. Making a scene will only ever escalate the issue.

When you have to work with people you don't know or are required to speak in front of an audience, staying calm will create a positive impression. It will help you keep your nerves in check, allowing you to interact or present with confidence. When you are calm, people are more likely listen to you and take action based on your words.

An effective calming strategy you can use anytime is to think about anxiety differently. If you frame it that you are feeling *excited* about, let's say a project, rather than feeling *anxious or nervous* about it, you are more likely to perform better and see positive results. Swapping out a negative word like "anxiety" for a simple, self-encouraging word like "excited" changes the scenario from overcoming a challenge to embracing an opportunity. The messages we feed ourselves every day, all day long, are frighteningly powerful and are always at work behind the scenes shaping our lives. When we worry about how things can go wrong, that's what we focus on. When we feel excited, we're focusing on what can go well. There's an old saying: "We are what we think." What we tell ourselves can make all the difference in how we get things done. I have used this technique in mediations, especially when parties are far away from a resolution. I shift away from the parties' anxieties and frustrations and approach them with the idea that settling can be an opportunity.

Moving beyond fear and anxiety

At the end of the day, you don't want to regret the chances you did not take because you were anxious or afraid of failure. Sometimes we feel as though we are the only person in the world with our issues. We need to embrace the fact that even the most famous, most accomplished, most admired people have fears, just as we do. The key is to learn how to manage those fears, facing them head-on with wisdom, calmness, and strength. Eleanor Roosevelt once said, "You gain strength, courage, and confidence by every experience in which you really stop to look fear in the face. You are able to say to yourself, 'I have lived through this horror. I can take the next thing that comes along.'"

To achieve calm in your life, you need to conquer your fears, practice self-compassion, stay strong, and build resilience. Prioritizing calm can improve your mental health and memory and protect your valuable time and your close relationships. Each of us will find different techniques that help us overcome fears and stay calm. For example, several years ago, I tried to overcome some of my fears (of heights, enclosed spaces, flying) by skydiving. Jumping out of a plane was the scariest thing I could think of, and I knew that facing that fear would teach me to face other fears and help change the narrative of my life. It did allow me to practice calming techniques, and I certainly felt more confident after I jumped!

There are so many ways to stay calm and get through difficult times. Always remember that your present situation is not your final destination, and sometimes the bad things that happen in our lives put us directly on the path to the best things that will ever happen to us. You don't have to have it all figured out to move forward. Recognize the people and situations that trigger stress and anxiety and try to understand what your limitations are. Be aware of the warning signs of stress like tension in your body, fatigue, insomnia, and irritability and figure out how you can respond to bring calm back into your life.

Psychotherapist Amy Morin, author of *13 Things Mentally Strong People Don't Do*, points out the key characteristics of a mentally strong person. They take responsibility for their actions and base their decisions on their own priorities and not the opinions of others. They admit when they're wrong, learn from their mistakes, and understand that regardless of the person they are today they can always be better. They focus on the bright side, celebrate the success of others, and make every minute count. They recognize their fears but don't allow their weaknesses to hold them back. And importantly, they maintain a balance between emotion and logical thinking and solve problems instead of complaining about them.

Two key steps on the path to staying calm are getting clear about what is really important and building resilience. Resilient people are able to stay calm and engage their active coping skills, which in turn helps them better manage conflict: they can take control, make a plan to improve the situation, and work toward it day by day. They build their courage, so they can cope better with fear and anxieties, and are able to challenge themselves, forging social connections and a support system along the way.

In "How to Build Resilience in Midlife," *New York Times* writer Tara Parker-Pope reviewed research on strengthening the ability to bounce back from adversity. She notes several ways to build resilience, including practicing optimism, rewriting your story, remembering your comebacks, supporting others, taking stress breaks, and going out of your comfort zone. Dennis Charney, resilience researcher and co-author of the book *Resilience: The Science of Mastering Life's Greatest Challenges,* is quoted in the article about the importance of resilience and the ability to overcome anxieties. He states that "your stress hormone systems will become less responsive to stress so you can handle stress better" when you do go out of your comfort zone and put yourself in challenging situations. Jack Groppel, co-founder of the Johnson & Johnson Human Performance Institute, is also quoted, advising us to recognize that we will never eliminate stress from our lives. Instead, we need to "create regular opportunities for the body to recover from stress"—such as taking a walk, meditating, or surrounding yourself with good friends.

How to be a calmer person

If you are somebody who is often worried or anxious and just generally feeling not so calm on the inside, how can you change? When I talk about being calm, I am not necessarily talking about your personality or your energy, or the things that people see on the outside. I'm talking about internally. How can you be calmer inside so that you feel less frazzled and less stressed out about everything that is going on in your life?

The first thing I do if I'm feeling like I really need to calm down is remove myself from the situation and do something that I know is going to get me back into a clear state of mind. For example, if something has completely thrown me off, instead of immediately responding—either by snapping at somebody or breaking down because I feel overwhelmed—I will go for a walk, listen to music, or even just watch a funny YouTube video, like bloopers from my favorite shows. These things let me get back to a right state of mind where I don't feel like I need to react right away. I think what makes us feel so overwhelmed is that we think we need to do something immediately. Sometimes we do, but often we don't.

The second thing that has helped me to become a calmer person is practicing meditation. I know that a lot of us overthinkers tend to shy away from meditation because there's this assumption that it's about clearing your mind and having zero thoughts. But the way I understand meditation, it is really about not reacting to your thoughts so much. I have found regular practice highly beneficial; I'll discuss it in more detail in the next section.

My third tip for bringing more calm into your life is actually a technique that you can use in the heat of the moment to diffuse a stressful situation. The next time you are feeling really anxious or worried about something, look for five things that you can see, four things that you can touch, three things that you can hear, two things that you can smell, and one thing that you can taste. It's a really great way to distract your mind from whatever it is focusing on (or overfocusing on) and is a wonderful grounding exercise for those moments when you feel anything but calm.

If you have a difficult time with your fears and anxieties, make sure you talk to someone you trust—a physician, a friend, a family member, or a counselor—who can help you devise a plan to overcome it. Sometimes life just gets too stressful and we need to prioritize self-care.

Simple ways to bring calm to your day

Making time to take care of yourself will allow you to show up for others more fully. Any activity that allows you to focus your attention inwardly or be more present in the moment can create greater satisfaction, increased calm, and more happiness.

Researchers at Harvard University found that the average person spends 46.9 percent of their days with their mind wandering. This research by psychologists Matthew Killingsworth and Daniel T. Gilbert, reported in *The Harvard Gazette*, "used an iPhone web app to gather 250,000 data points on subjects' thoughts, feelings, and actions as they went about their lives." They found that "a human mind is a wandering mind, and a wandering mind is an unhappy mind. . . . The ability to think about what is not happening is a cognitive achievement that comes at an emotional cost."

Meditation is a way to quiet and focus your mind whenever you need to achieve some semblance of calm. I have to admit, the idea that it could help seemed incomprehensible to me a few months ago, but friends had recommended it enthusiastically and I felt I needed to try it out. At first, my mind would wander and I found myself thinking about all the tasks I needed to complete that day. Eventually, I was able to meditate for five to ten minutes at a time several times a week. Mediation has made me better at focusing my attention and calms me so I can be better prepared for whatever the day may bring. The more you practice it, the easier it becomes.

Mindfulness is another popular calming technique; it involves bringing your awareness to the present moment. You can practice mindfulness as you go about your day, or in a more focused way if that helps. You might try sitting in a quiet place and concentrating on a certain feeling or sense you are experiencing or doing an activity that calms your nerves, such as knitting, puzzles, reading, or taking a walk. You could also schedule times to take a mindfulness break by doing something you enjoy, like walking, cooking, or gardening, with extra focus and care.

If you find you have too much conflict in your life, find ways to avoid it, including walking away if you need to. Schedule time for five-minute meditations or some other calming technique at least every other day. List your three biggest fears and possible ways to overcome them. Write down ways to add calm and eliminate stress in your life, using simple strategies you can practice regularly, at least once a week.

Any kind of exercise can alleviate stress. There are countless options, from home videos and equipment to classes at nearby gyms and studios. Exercising is an effective way to deal with anxieties and maintain a healthy lifestyle, but sometimes you need a little help to get started and keep going. There is ample evidence that getting support from others can encourage you to stick to your exercise routine. There are teams you can join, like running teams, which are offered at every level. There are races and tournaments, challenges to enter that will motivate you to stick to a fitness schedule. There are apps to help you get started on a program, interact with others, and challenge yourself. One app called Charity Miles even allows you to earn money for a favorite charity based on each mile you walk, run, or bike.

Years ago, I needed some motivation to get in shape and I wanted a big challenge, so I signed up for a half marathon. This pushed me to research training methods and keep to a schedule of days, times, and miles. It helped that I also told family and friends of my plans, since I knew I would not want to disappoint them or, more importantly, myself. I completed my first half marathon on schedule, then followed it up with a few others before eventually running a full marathon. Training let me get in shape and alleviated day-to-day stress. Running was a tool that allowed me to cope with my own anxieties.

Staying calm under pressure

Whether you are preparing for an interview, a speech, or an important meeting, it is imperative to come up with ways to stay calm under pressure. When I'm in difficult, high-pressure situations I'm prone to overreacting. Under such stress, I know I perform better when I have skills in my toolbox that will allow me to calm my nerves quickly.

Here are some strategies I have found useful that can help you cope with stress and stay calm:

- Take a break when you anticipate a stressful time. Engage in an activity that you enjoy like doing a crossword puzzle, playing a game, drawing, reading, stretching, knitting, or going for a walk. I try to calm down by listening to music, doing a sudoku puzzle, or reading a book or magazine.
- Participate in mindful practice. Take a moment and visualize yourself in a calm environment. This mindful moment will give you a better perspective and enable you to ignore distractions and distance yourself from potential conflicts.
- Be honest about the things that give you anxiety or stress. Once you admit to these feelings, you can face them and find ways to avoid and negate them.
- Challenge your thoughts. I know I have a fear of flying, so I challenge my fears by reviewing safety facts before getting on a plane.
- Distract yourself. Take a walk, call a friend, or even count to ten—anything that will reset your brain for a moment so you can let go and get back on track.
- Replace the stress. Visualize something that makes you feel happy and relaxed. If you anticipate a stressful time or have just finished dealing with a hectic situation, take a run, do a workout, spend time with a friend or family member, finish writing a card, or volunteer your time for a good cause. Doing

something that will replace the stress can make you feel better.

- Learn how massaging your body's pressure points can calm your anxieties. Go to a massage therapist or do it to yourself. I have a back massager that I get out when I'm feeling anxious.

- Have a centering object like a piece of jewelry, stuffed animal, ball, or rock that you can touch when you are anxious. In times of stress, I wear my grandmother's ring. I organized a project with friends where we created rocks with different positive sayings or drawings. These rocks have been used as centering objects by many friends and have helped them focus. I keep a few in my bathroom to look at when I'm having a stressful day.

- Avoid situations and people that make you anxious or stressed. Do not surround yourself with negative people, especially when you have an important event or activity. If you are about to make a big presentation, call people who will be positive.

- Before you go into a difficult situation, practice different responses to what you anticipate. As an attorney, I practiced a lot before going to court. This would allow me to avoid exaggerated, aggressive, and emotional responses. Aim for calm, thoughtful, and assertive instead.

- Learn breathing exercises. Taking a deep breath can help you stay calm. Or, even better, take some time to learn how to breathe properly. Shallow breathing means that the diaphragm muscles are not being used. The secret is to inhale deeply so that the chest is filled with air. If you are lying down, you can easily feel your stomach rising as the diaphragm drops by placing your hands over your belly button. Then exhale slowly. As you do, concentrate on the movement you feel; you can also repeat a mantra such as "Breathe in" and "Breathe out." There are numerous apps that can teach you this technique, such as Breathe, Calm, and Headspace.

- Regularly practicing meditation can help when you are in stressful situations; it will teach you how to observe your surroundings without reacting to them. Whether it's a careless driver, slow-moving colleague, or anything else, try not to react, stay calm, and let go of the situation.

- Ask for guidance from a professional or a friend you trust. There is nothing wrong with asking for help; it is beneficial for everyone to talk to others about their frustrations, fears, and anxieties. If you want to reach out to a professional, ask for recommendations from a trusted friend or go to the American Psychological Association's Psychologist Locator website (locator. apa.org) to find someone near you.

- Keep a journal and write down your feelings and experiences. Writing helps many let go of anxieties and concerns.

- Take care of yourself by sleeping right, exercising, and eating well. Get into some regular practices that will allow you to feel better, handle different kinds of situations, and put things into perspective.

- Before you go to sleep each day, write a list of everything that is on your mind, including your concerns, your to-do list, or the people you need to call. Emptying your mind onto a piece of paper can provide you with some semblance of calm before you go to sleep. Other sleep suggestions include setting an alarm every night to tell you when to go to bed, sticking to regular bedtimes, and avoiding screen time for up to an hour before you sleep. The Calm app offers one hundred hours of content to help you get rid of pending anxieties and fall asleep faster.

Many of my fears and anxieties have centered on my children and their safety and well-being. Over time, I realized for their sake and mine that I need to come up with appropriate tools to relieve some of these anxieties. One of the things that worked to lower my overall anxiety was to make a bucket list and complete all the items on it, including some that caused me tremendous fear. (Remember the skydiving?) I also brought more exercise and meditation into my life and worked to accept that there are only certain things I can control.

I recently sent a diagram to my children that listed the things they can and can't control. The list of things that they can control included:

- Working hard, doing their homework, and studying for tests
- Respecting property
- Being kind
- Being accountable
- Choosing certain friends
- Making certain decisions
- Forgiving and apologizing
- Choosing how to respond to challenges
- Trying again
- How they spend their free time
- Being honest

- Taking care of themselves
- Asking for help
- How they respond to others

The things that they can't control include:

- Someone else's decisions
- Death
- Who likes them
- How others take care of themselves
- How others treat them
- Others being kind
- Others apologizing or forgiving them
- Others being honest
- Past mistakes
- Height
- Looks
- The weather

Making a list of the things you can control and things that you can't, will let you see things more clearly, set aside some of your anxieties, and achieve more calm.

You must learn to let go. Release the stress. You were never in control anyway.

–STEVE MARABOLI

SEVEN ACTION STEPS TO CREATE MORE CALM

1. Take good care of your mind and body. Eat well, sleep well, and exercise—it's so important.

2. Learn relaxation tools that you can use when things get a little crazy. Practice these steps so you are prepared to use them when a stressful situation arises. Techniques such as deep breathing can help you in the heat of the moment, while meditation, yoga, and mindfulness make you calmer in general.

3. Before going to sleep, make a quick list of things to do and decisions to be made either the next day or within the next week. Sometimes putting them on paper can allow you to clear them from your mind.

4. If you are anticipating a stressful situation, practice some simple self-care techniques beforehand to put yourself in a calmer frame of mind.

5. When you feel anxious about something, try not to fixate on aspects of the situation that are out of your control. Making a list of the things you can control and the things you can't, will help to put things in perspective.

6. Take a step away whenever you get anxious or become overwhelmed by conflict. Avoid being reactive and have a go-to technique you can use to bring back your sense of calm.

7. If you are struggling to let go of your anxiety, fears, and worries, consider reaching out and talking to someone. Sometimes just saying things out loud can release the pressure and make you feel better.

THOUGHTS AND ACTIONS TOWARD MORE CALM

What makes you calm?

What do you do to combat anxiety, anger, fear, or frustration?

How do you handle conflict?

Write down three action steps you will schedule on your calendar:
Some ideas include creating an exercise routine, researching ways to address conflict, writing down fears or anxieties, participating in some kind of calming exercises or meditations, and scheduling time for a stress break a few times a week.

1.

2.

3.

MORE THOUGHTS

MORE CALM

_____

_____

_____

_____

_____

_____

_____

_____

_____

_____

_____

_____

_____

_____

_____

MORE

_____

_____

_____

_____

_____

_____

_____

_____

_____

_____

_____

_____

_____

_____

CHAPTER 7

More Success

Success is nothing more than a few simple disciplines, practiced every day.

–JIM ROHN

If you talk about it, it's a dream. If you envision it, it's possible. If you schedule it, it's real.

–TONY ROBBINS

Success can mean different things to different people. For some, it could be losing twenty pounds. For others, it could be reaching a sales goal at work. And for others, it could be getting a certain job, owning a home, running a business, or hosting a charity event. Depending on your values and life situation, success can be measured by the number of material possessions you own, or what your children do, or the house you live in, or the car you drive. According to Richard Branson, we should measure success by how happy we are, not by how much money we make or whom we associate with. My definition of success has changed throughout my life as I have reached different milestones. Today, success is a compilation of professional and personal achievements, this book, and, most importantly, the relationships I have built and the way I have impacted others.

I recently read a *People* magazine article about a homeless teen, Chelesea Fearce, who decided she wanted her life to be different. She defined success as not having to live in shelters, cars, or hotels. She remembers thinking, "In order to get out of this situation, I'm going to need tools." She returned to school and excelled. With the support of scholarships, she graduated from college and is now a student at the Yale School of Medicine. "You can't get stuck in the moment . . . you always have to think about your future and what inspires you. That's helped me get through," she says. "You can accomplish anything you want, you just need to keep your eye on the prize."

There are countless articles that document the success stories of others. I've read about people who lost weight and got in shape—that was their success story. There are others who consider themselves successful because they achieved an athletics goal, succeeded in getting to the C-suite, found fame in entertainment, have felt rewarded by their work or by their success in running a business or household. There are those who define success by their volunteer work. Many define success by a mixture of the above. What I do know is that *each person needs to define their own success*. Whatever situation you are in, only you can define your goals and purpose and what succeeding in them will look like.

Finding motivation

Even the most ambitious people sometimes struggle with motivation. I have always looked for new ways to get motivated, especially during difficult and stressful times. Whenever I'm struggling with self-doubt, I make an effort to learn and read about the powerful success stories of others to help me focus on my goals and build determination. When I need some extra motivation, I'll often look to my collection of quotes, both serious and funny; here are some of my favorites:

- "I have not failed. I've just found ten thousand ways that won't work." Attributed to *Thomas Edison*
- "Nothing is impossible; the word itself says 'I'm possible!'" *Audrey Hepburn*
- "Change the way you look at things, and the things you look at change." *Wayne W. Dyer*
- "Opportunity is missed by most people because it is dressed in overalls and looks like work." Attributed to *Thomas Edison*
- "You must learn from the mistakes of others. You can't possibly live long enough to make them all yourself." *Attributed to Sam Levenson*
- "Never doubt that a small group of thoughtful, committed citizens can change the world. Indeed, it is the only thing that ever has." *Margaret Mead*
- "Sometimes life knocks you (down) . . . get up, get up, get up!!! Happiness is not the absence of problems—it's the ability to deal with them." *Steve Maraboli*

It is easy to find a quote or a story that will inspire you on your road to success. Find one that appeals to you and tape it to your mirror, on your refrigerator, or in your office. Choose a place where you'll see it and be reminded (especially on the bad and unproductive days) that you have goals to attain.

There are countless stories of people who have found success by working hard, being innovative, and fulfilling the needs of other people. Their success entailed a lot of work and sacrifice, but with the right ideas and opportunities, they achieved their goals. Pierre Omidyar, a computer programmer, began auctioning his belongings online in 1995. While AuctionWeb began as a personal project, it grew exponentially. In a few short years, he had upgraded to a business account, started charging fees, and hired an employee to manage the web traffic. His site is now known as eBay. Matt Maloney and Mike Evans were working as software developers in Chicago and found themselves frustrated by the lack of decent restaurants offering delivery or takeout. So they solved their own problem and created a one-stop shop for food delivery, GrubHub. Today, their company has gone public and is valued at more than $3 billion. Joe Coulombe was operating a small chain of convenience stores in southern California when it struck him that his college-educated clientele were looking for something better than the basic 7-Eleven-style takeaway food options on offer. He opened a tropical-themed market in Pasadena that was well stocked with food and beverages served by friendly staff. It was a hit, so he expanded, adding healthy food options and opening up at locations near universities—and that was the beginning of Trader Joe's.

You can find inspiring examples of success in every field imaginable. I have met with or heard about Olympic and Paralympic athletes, professionals, homemakers, activists, teachers, community leaders, and many others who have defined and achieved their own successes. Each story provides inspiration and is living proof that the world is full of infinite possibilities and countless opportunities for those who have a passion, a dream, and are willing to put in the work to make it happen.

For those of us who are a little bit older, ideas of success may include reinvention. This book was a goal that I set as I approached my fifties and was looking for ways to reinvent myself and give back to others the many lessons I have learned. Reinvention has allowed me to explore different opportunities and grow personally—it's never too late to create a new vision of success for yourself. Recently, I read *Comeback Careers: Rethink, Refresh, Reinvent Your Success—at 40, 50, and Beyond* by Mika Brzezinski and Ginny Brzezinski. They interviewed many career-changers working in a variety of fields to show that career reinvention is possible at any age. They share successful relaunchers' secrets to overcoming obstacles, both internal and external, and their step-by-step processes, strategies, and candid advice for others reinventing themselves.

You can only become truly accomplished at something you love. Don't make money your goal. Instead, pursue the things you love doing, and then do them so well that people can't take their eyes off of you.

—MAYA ANGELOU

Setting goals sets you up for success

However one defines success, setting attainable goals is important to maintaining a sense of purpose and happiness. You can work toward your goals effectively when they are specific, measurable, challenging, and driven by your desires and values. Having a goal makes you feel optimistic about your future and gives you self-confidence about your abilities and your worth. It lets you feel accomplished and proud and encourages good habits.

So why is goal setting important? It gives you a list of manageable steps that you can follow to take your life from where it is now to where you want it to be. Creating goals can be the defining factor in whether or not we achieve our definitions of personal and professional success. Goals provide you with something tangible to aim for that will help you to continue moving forward in the right direction. Without them, we lack focus and purpose, wasting time, energy, and effort. Setting goals keeps you accountable, lets you measure your progress, and allows you to reevaluate and make adjustments when necessary. Having some clearly defined goals will make you feel better about yourself, especially when you focus on those goals, actively work toward them, and achieve what you set forth to accomplish.

Goal setting also makes our dreams seem within reach. By breaking big goals down into smaller, manageable chunks, we can more easily build and maintain the momentum we need. When you make small, continual progress each day, you will slowly transition into the person you want to become. Our time on this earth is limited, and setting clearly defined goals can ensure that you make the most of your life and live it to the fullest.

We all have talents and ambitions; setting goals that align with them has the potential to take us to some amazing places. To achieve your biggest dreams, you need to be willing to sit down and design a life uniquely tailored to you that will allow you to achieve them.

The SMART way to set goals

It is essential that goals be clearly defined and easy to follow. The SMART technique is a system used around the world as a focused, effective framework for setting goals. Although variations of this system had been in use for decades, the acronym first appeared in a 1981 article by George T. Doran, a business consultant and executive.

To use the SMART technique, you write your goals in a way that addresses each of the five SMART criteria:

1. **Specific.** First and foremost, your goal must be specific. Use clear and concise language to define why you want to achieve your goal, who will help you accomplish it, what exactly you need to do, where the work will take place, and when it should be completed.
2. **Measurable.** It's important to have a measurable outcome for your goal so there are no gray areas; adding specific numbers or details to your plan is a must. Doing so will let you track your results, make any necessary adjustments as you go, and enable you to measure your overall success.
3. **Attainable.** While big dreams are always encouraged, when it comes to setting goals they must be attainable— but not so easily that they don't present a challenge. Striking the right balance is key to your chances of success.
4. **Relevant.** Your goal must be meaningful and important to you, right now. This is critical, as it is ultimately what will motivate you to push on during difficult moments. When your goal is aligned with your values and purpose, achieving it is worth every bit of the effort.

5. **Time-bound.** Your goal will also need a deadline to provide you with the sense of urgency that gets it off your to-do list and onto your daily agenda. With a clear time frame in front of you, you'll feel motivated to keep chipping away so you can stay on track.

The SMART system makes goal setting much easier—and makes you much more likely to succeed. Of course you still need to put in the hard work required to get to the finish line, but with the path clearly mapped out, you can focus your efforts and stick it out to the end.

There are other methods of mapping out your goals, including the FAST system, introduced by management experts Donald and Charles Sull. They found that four core principles underpin effective goal systems and summarized these elements with the acronym FAST. According to their article in the *MIT Sloan Management Review,* "Goals should be embedded in **frequent** discussions; **ambitious** in scope; measured by **specific** metrics and milestones; and be **transparent** for everyone . . . to see." Whether you want to work SMART or FAST, or invent an acronym of your own, setting goals will be the first and most important step toward more success.

It all starts with a vision

Tony Robbins is an inspiring example of personal success. He travels constantly but still manages fifty-four businesses that gross more than $6 billion in annual sales. He also hosts seminars that help millions of people become their best selves, spends time with his family, and acts as a personal advisor for celebrities and politicians across the United States.

So how does he do it? He says that regardless of what you are striving to achieve, you need to start by creating a vision. In an article in the December 3, 2018, issue of *Success* magazine, Robbins talks about how becoming the person you want to be is not hard if you have the dedication, focus, and tools you need.

First, Robbins points out, you should always set your sights on something within reason. "Most people overestimate what they're going to do in a year, and they underestimate what they can do in a decade, or two or three or four," he says.

He recommends a five-step plan to attaining your goals, which involves feeding your mind, strengthening your body, finding a great role model, taking action, and "getting outside of yourself" so your goals are not just about you but also add value to others.

To start the process of setting your goals and achieving them, Robbins suggests you ask yourself these six questions: "What am I here to serve? What is my core passion? What resources are available to me? What do I need to change in myself? What is my how? How can I implement this?" Think carefully about how you will answer all of these questions, and then make your plan and set it in motion.

There are several methods that can help you create a vision. The goal is to imagine yourself three to five years in the future in as much detail as possible. You can actually paint a vivid picture of what you desire. You can also use a dream or vision board, a visual tool that brings together pictures or symbols of what you want to allow you to define and focus on a significant life goal or a desired future. At the beginning of every school year, I bring in boards, magazines, pictures, and supplies to help the girls I mentor create vision boards of their own. This activity gives them an opportunity to visualize their dreams; they keep their boards in a prominent place at home so they can constantly be reminded of their goals and inspired to reach for them.

The power of a growth mindset and positive attitude

Every year, millions of people make resolutions, yet most fail to realize their goals. What stands in the way? Usually, a person's own mindset, attitude, or self-perception will stifle their ability to reach their goals. Staying positive and fostering self-belief is critical to success.

> Nothing can stop the man with the right mental attitude from achieving his goal; nothing on earth can help the man with the wrong mental attitude.
> **–ATTRIBUTED TO THOMAS JEFFERSON**

Staying positive can change the way you approach obstacles and problems. Instead of being negative, think confidently about how you will accomplish the task at hand. With a positive outlook, it's much easier to overcome your challenges. While it's OK to have doubts and uncertainty regarding your goals and resolutions, if you find yourself slipping toward negativity, seek out supportive people or use other strategies that will steer you back toward a positive frame of mind. There will always be setbacks, doubts, distractions, and frustrations—but with the right mindset, anything is possible.

Psychologist Carol Dweck distinguishes between a fixed mindset and a growth mindset. A fixed mindset is when we believe our talents, personality, and intelligence are unchangeable traits. We are smart and capable or we're not. People with a growth mindset believe that their most basic abilities can be developed through dedication and hard work, that brains and gifts are just the start. This viewpoint creates a love of learning and, even more importantly, a resilience that is critical to any new endeavor.

One of the secrets to personal growth is deliberate practice. It involves four steps. First, set small realistic goals. Second, stay the course. Third, measure your progress. And fourth, recharge your batteries. Entrepreneur Michael Simmons spent a year exploring the personal histories of business leaders—including Oprah Winfrey, Bill Gates, Elon Musk, Mark Zuckerberg, and Warren Buffett—to discover how they engage in deliberate practice. He found that despite their hectic schedules, they all set aside about five hours each week to learn and practice their craft. They do this consistently, and that deliberate practice plays a big part in their ongoing success. Even leaders of the past used deliberate practice; Benjamin Franklin's strict daily schedule included time for learning, reflection, and reading.

Growth can come from many other places. In *The Book of Mistakes: 9 Secrets to Creating a Successful Future*, author Skip Prichard discusses the need to get out of your comfort zone, read about different issues, and be open to different people, connections, and ideas. He believes that the connections we make with other people really fuel our own success. At the same time, he cautions that one of the biggest mistakes is allowing someone else to define your value; you limit your potential when you look for external validation. Prichard emphasizes the importance of thinking about the labels that you want to be known for; getting rid of old, outgrown labels, and really accepting your value.

Daily habits for success

One way you can get better about setting goals and achieving them successfully is to enlist the help of your friends. Several years ago, I created a circle of trust with two friends, where we discuss our goals and keep one another accountable.

There are other ways to ensure more success. Make a habit of celebrating your achievements; this reinforcement will give you the strength and attitude to move forward to the next goal. Find a great role model to show you how someone else found the road to success. Accept that your own approval is enough. Learn from your mistakes. Be OK with setbacks. You are only human; don't be so hard on yourself.

Persistence is vital to achieving your goals. Many of the most successful people I know demonstrate the power of persistence in both their personal and professional lives. My brother's fraternity had to memorize this quote attributed to Calvin Coolidge (a founding member of the organization): "Nothing in this world can take the place of persistence. Talent will not; nothing is more common than unsuccessful men with talent. Genius will not; unrewarded genius is almost a proverb. Education will not; the world is full of educated derelicts. Persistence and determination alone are omnipotent. The slogan Press On! has solved and always will solve the problems of the human race."

Success doesn't come from what you do occasionally, it comes from what you do consistently.

–MARIE FORLEO

Changing bad habits—or habits you have outgrown—can also spur success. Some people say it's too hard to change. But according to many sources, it takes just twenty-one days. There are many resources that can help you if old habits are holding you back. Author James Clear describes the four stages of creating a new habit— cue, craving, response, and reward—in his book *Atomic Habits*. He believes that changing your life is about creating new habits rather than making big breakthroughs. Clear's work expands on the theories behind habits formulated by Charles Duhigg in *The Power of Habit*, in which he explains how habits work and provides strategies and practical techniques to create change on an individual, organizational, and societal level.

Other people say it's too late to change or they're too old. But I know many people in their forties, fifties, and sixties who are achieving new goals. This book is a perfect example of a goal I wanted to attain. There were a million reasons why I shouldn't do it, but I set my goal and I made it happen.

Reading can be another helpful tool in your search for more success. Tom Corley, accountant, financial planner, and author of *Change your Habits, Change your Life*, surveyed 233 wealthy individuals and found they had one daily habit in common: reading. Eighty-eight percent of the individuals said they read at least thirty minutes a day. Make sure you read every day, even if it's just for a few minutes, and schedule time for reading regularly in your calendar.

There are lots of other ways to help achieve your goals. If you have a hard time getting things done because you are a perfectionist or you can't make decisions, give yourself a deadline and accept that nobody is perfect. Try not to overcommit to too many goals at once. Set attainable goals. Ask a coach, friend, or colleague to support you. Schedule time every week where you put away possible distractions like your phone and focus on getting things done, scheduling what needs to get done, and making a plan for how you'll succeed. Become an active learner. Focus on changing one habit at a time, starting with your morning routines. And don't give up!

Getting unstuck

Many times in my life, I have felt stuck and wasn't sure how to proceed. Almost everyone I know has felt stuck at some point. Whether you are pivoting in an existing career or starting something new, there will always be challenges and insecurities. Sometimes it has been difficult for me to stay motivated and focused, especially when gearing up for a new challenge I'm uncertain about. If you feel stuck and need help, reach out to a coach, friend, colleague, or mentor. With their support, you should be able to set different goals and find ways to focus on achieving them.

Planning and scheduling your actions in your calendar, noting when you will do what and how, is another effective way to get back on track. Review how each day went, and what you learned, so you can build and improve. Look to the examples of others who have achieved the kind of success you are striving for by reading books, magazines, relevant journals, and researching online.

If you are struggling to focus, eliminate any distractions that are getting in your way. It may help to write a list of your personal distractions. Are you paying too much attention to social media or emails? I find myself watching a favorite show or organizing a closet when I should be focusing on the task at hand. Allocate a separate time for these distractions and hold yourself accountable for avoiding them at all other times. When I worked on this book, I would put my phone in another room, eliminating that potent distraction for a period of time.

Self-doubt can be disruptive and hurtful, especially when you are trying to move out of your comfort zone, so if this is an issue for you, create coping mechanisms that will let you deal with your anxieties and fears, including many of those I wrote about in chapter 6. Admit that it is OK to experience these feelings, and experiment with different methods to control or overcome them. Close your eyes, meditate, or just take deep breaths to help you focus.

It's important to be positive, creative, and enjoy the journey as much as you can. Take a break when you are feeling unmotivated. You may need to set aside time for fun and relaxing activities. If you need a boost, schedule time with family and friends and do something, anything, that makes you happy.

The secret of success: A story

"Sir, What is the secret of your success?" a reporter asked a bank president.

"Two words."

"And sir, what are they?"

"Right decisions."

"And sir, how do you make right decisions?"

"One word."

"And sir, what is that?"

"Experience."

"And sir, how do you get experience?"

"Two words"

"And sir, what are they?"
"Wrong decisions."

A huge part of success is failure. Overcoming setbacks and rejection is an important element of success. Author J.K. Rowling, the world's first billionaire author, has sold more than 500 million copies of her Harry Potter books and they have been made into hugely successful films. She has been interviewed many times and has told people that her success would not have been possible without years of epic failure. At twenty-eight, she was a single mother struggling to survive. She did not have a job, had no money, and considered herself "the biggest failure I knew." The first Harry Potter book was rejected by twelve publishers before it was finally accepted. At her 2008 commencement speech at Harvard she said, "Failure taught me things about myself that I could have learned no other way. I discovered that I had a strong will, and more discipline than I had suspected." She said, "It is impossible to live without failing at something, unless you live so cautiously that you might as well not have lived at all—in which case, you fail by default."

My family watched the ESPN series *The Last Dance*, which documents the professional career of Michael Jordan, specifically his last year as a basketball phenomenon at the Chicago Bulls. He is widely considered to be the best basketball player of all time. However, that was not always the case—in his sophomore year of high school, he tried out for the varsity basketball team but was told he was too short and didn't make the team.

Oprah Winfrey has spoken publicly many times about her struggles and failures. She has revealed that she was born to a single teenage mother and was exposed to childhood abuse.

Despite her desire to become a news anchor, she was fired from her first job for being "unfit for television news." She was told that she couldn't keep her emotions out of her stories. As you know, she later had one of the most successful careers in television and eventually became one of the most influential people in the world.

Walt Disney's first company, Laugh-O-Gram Films, eventually failed and went bankrupt. He was fired from *The Kansas City Star* because he "lacked imagination and had no good ideas." For years, he struggled until he founded Disney and created some of the world's favorite characters like Mickey Mouse and Donald Duck and one of my kids' favorite places, Walt Disney World. Disney and its huge outreach and success is a tribute to Walt Disney and his creativity, determination, and ability to overcome failure and rejection.

There are countless other stories of failure, including Steven Spielberg being denied admission to the University of Southern California School of Cinematic Arts three times and Henry Ford failing twice and going bankrupt before launching the Ford Motor Company. Elvis Presley performed for the first time at the Grand Ole Opry and was told he should go back to driving trucks. Even Thomas Edison failed to invent the lightbulb ten thousand times before he got it right.

The website Weightlifting for a Beautiful World published the findings of a 2016 study. "Researchers at the Teachers College of Columbia University asked three different groups of high school students to read the biographies of three very famous scientists: Marie Curie, Albert Einstein, and Michael Faraday. One of the groups read biographies that . . . focused totally on the accomplishments of the scientists. However, the other two groups read biographies that . . . focused primarily on their personal and their professional struggles, including foiled ambitions and some experiments that had failed. The students who read about the scientists' struggles went on to perform better in math and science classes." The researchers concluded that "the message that even successful scientists experience failures prior to their achievements may help students interpret their difficulties in science classes as normal occurrences rather than a reflection of their lack of intelligence or talent for science."

At the end of the day, only you can define your success. Use the success of others in your field as inspiration and learn from your failures and the failures of others. Be strategic and use the resources available to keep yourself motivated to achieve your goals, whatever they may be. Don't get too caught up with failure, but do learn from it. Don't do this alone; ask for help when you need it. Don't compare yourself to others. Everyone's life experiences and desires are different; don't allow others to define your success for you.

What is success to you?

Remember to consider what success means to you. Success means different things to different people. For some people, it could mean a certain amount of power or wealth. For others, it could be obtaining a certain position in their place of work. For others, it could be a particular impact they want to have in the world. Success may be defined by some through the achievements of their children, significant others, or certain friends and family members. Success can be finishing a race, discovering a new talent, or even writing a book. Figure out what success is to you. It can entail different accomplishments and can change over time. Success is unique to each individual.

It is imperative to understand that despite all of the expert advice, books, and articles that are available, you need to focus on what is relevant to your life, personality, and style. Following advice that you can't relate to will just create disappointment and failure. Research different paths to success and proceed with what feels right to you. Match your strengths with the right techniques and you will find more success in everything you do.

SEVEN ACTION STEPS
TO CREATE MORE SUCCESS

1. Come up with a plan—be strategic with your thoughts and time. Every success starts with a thoughtful vision.

2. Analyze your strengths and weaknesses. There are several methods to assess your capabilities and identify possible changes. One tool we have used is Strengths Finder, but there are several personality assessments that can provide you with insight.

3. Keep learning more to allow yourself to expand and grow. Read, read, read!

4. Practice self-care. Plan regularly to spend time with those you love and do things you enjoy.

5. Write down your goals and use the SMART method or another framework to ensure they are actionable and achievable.

6. Enlist an accountability coach, friend, or colleague to help you stay focused on achieving your goals.

7. Don't keep your goals a secret. Tell your supportive friends and family so they can cheer you on.

THOUGHTS AND ACTIONS TOWARD MORE SUCCESS

How do you define success?

What goals would you like to accomplish?

How do you celebrate your successes?

Write down three action steps you will schedule on your calendar:
Some ideas include setting attainable goals, getting an accountability coach or friend, scheduling time every week to focus on making a plan for the future, improving certain habits, and learning about something that has always interested you.

1.

2.

3.

MORE THOUGHTS

MORE SUCCESS

_____

_____

_____

_____

_____

_____

_____

_____

_____

_____

_____

_____

_____

_____

MORE

Epilogue

Since I started putting this book together, I have been quarantined with my husband and children because of the spread of COVID-19. During this time, we have cried, laughed, and experienced the highs and lows of life together. We have struggled with moments of anxiety, health scares, business interruptions, occasional squabbles, and tragic loss, even attending funerals via Zoom. In between virtual classes and business meetings, we have also been fortunate to have some incredible and special moments including game days, walks around the neighborhood with our dog, completing puzzles, deep conversations, cleaning out, revisiting old memories, ping-pong tournaments, movie nights, and so much more. We even attended life celebrations via Zoom and drive-bys. Thankfully, we also had the ability to give back to others in need. I'm not sure how things will change in the post-coronavirus world, but I do know that it is never too late to make changes. For me, I need to appreciate the little things and remember I can always do more. "We may not have it all together but together we have it all" seems like an appropriate way to explain this time. This opportunity, despite all the grief, has made it even more apparent that I need to make the most of every day.

My brother and mom had COVID-19 and wound up in ICU because of their escalating and life-threatening symptoms. Thankfully, they both survived and are healthy. I asked them what changed for them during this time. My brother gave me this quote by Leigh Weinraub on mindfulness: "Don't sweat the small stuff, smell the roses, and live life. Help family more. Love is the vaccine to all. Choose Love! Use love in any capacity you can." He also quoted Al Gore: "The single most important choice that any of us make as individuals and as a society is between the hard right and the easy wrong." My mom said she is so grateful for our family. She feels blessed to "live so close to the family and share in their lives; the pleasure of joy that I get when I cook, share dinners, share my love of art; and being there for each other when needed." Their experiences not only changed their outlook on life but had a huge impact on me and all who know and love them. I have realized with more clarity that life can be short, which has made it even more important to share this book with everyone.

⁂

When I started this project years ago, it was a way to organize my thoughts, ideas, and anecdotes inspired by others and my own experiences. I want to finish it with some of my favorite lessons, which include:

- Stay positive—learn how to deal with disappointment. It is the best weapon against internal and external threats.
- Be grateful for anything and everything.

- Be persistent and work hard.
- Realize that failure is not always a bad thing.
- Build a network of friends and colleagues who bring positivity and strength into your life.
- Always learn and try to improve yourself, including finding ways to stay calm in moments of anxiety, anger, or frustration.
- Organize your life and create balance.
- Cut out bad habits like apologizing all the time, obsessing over what others do, and playing it safe.
- Create a vision, plan for the next few years, and have the confidence to move forward.
- Don't sweat the small stuff.

While writing this book, I have tried to change my own bad habits by being more patient, kinder, appreciating the little things, and cherishing my loved ones. I implore my family and friends, and now my readers, to join me on this journey of MORE. Problems can seem insurmountable and goals inaccessible, but anything and everything is possible.

During one of my cycling classes, my instructor, Robin, told us, "I am not here to exist. I'm here to love, live, and thrive." She also said, "You are one limited edition." This struck me as being so consistent with the themes of my book. *More* is not about the pressure to be perfect. It's just simply about trying to get everything out of life. Only you can decide what is lacking in your life and what you aspire to improve. Once you do, there are countless resources and people who can help you to achieve your goals. We only get one life, and I have made it my mission to make the most of it, and to help my children, family, friends, colleagues, and the readers of this book to do the same.

MORE

Ask yourself, What more would you like to get out of this life?

More gratitude? More success? More balance? More calm?

Make that decision, marshal your resources, and then take one step at a time to achieve the more we all deserve.

References

Quotes—I have been collecting quotes for years from lots of different sources. Some had identified authors, while some authors were unknown. Some have been in circulation so long, their origin has become unclear or their attribution confused. I have done my best to track down authorship when I can and attribute the quotes correctly.

Achor, Shawn. 2019. "Surround Yourself With These Positive Influencers." *Success*, March 1, 2019. Accessed September 18, 2020. https://www.success.com/positive-influencers/.

Ackerman, Courtney E. 2020. "What is Positive Mindset: 89 Ways to Achieve a Positive Mental Attitude." *Positive Psychology.* January 9, 2020. Accessed September 18, 2020. https://positivepsychology.com/positive-mindset/.

Allen, Summer. 2018. "The Science of Generosity." Greater Good Science Center at UC Berkeley. Accessed September 18, 2020. https://ggsc.berkeley.edu/images/uploads/GGSC-JTF_White_Paper-Generosity-FINAL.pdf.

Anik, Lalin, Aknin, Lara B, Norton, Michael I, Dunn, and Elizabeth W. 2009. "Feeling Good about Giving: The Benefits (and Costs) of Self-Interested Charitable Behavior." Harvard Business School. Accessed September 18, 2020. https://www.hbs.edu/faculty/Publication%20Files/10-012_0350a55d-585b-419d-89e7-91833a612fb5.pdf.

Best Self Journal and Planner. 2020. Accessed September 18, 2020. www.BestSelf Co.

Bureau of Labor Statistics, "American Time Use Survey — 2019 Results." June 25, 2020. Accessed September 18, 2020. https://www.bls.gov/news.release/pdf/atus.pdf.

Bradberry, Travis. 2020. "How Complaining Rewires Your Brain For Negativity." TalentSmart. Accessed September 18, 2020. https://www.talentsmart.com/articles/How-Complaining-Rewires-Your-Brain-for-Negativity-2147446676-p-1.html.

Bradberry, Travis, and Graves, Jean. 2009. *Emotional Intelligence 2.0*. San Diego: TalentSmart.

Brzezinski, Mika and Brzezinski, Ginny. 2020. *Comeback Careers: Rethink, Refresh, Reinvent Your Success—At 40, 50, and Beyond*. New York: Hachette Books.

Cacioppo, John T, and Cacioppo, Stephanie. 2018. "The Growing Problem of Loneliness." Lancet, 391, no. 10119 (February): 426. https://www.ncbi.nlm.nih.gov/pmc/articles/PMC6530780/.

Chamine, Shirzad. 2012. *Positive Intelligence: Why Only 20% of Teams and Individuals Achieve Their True Potential AND HOW YOU CAN ACHIEVE YOURS*. Austin, TX: Greenleaf Book Group Press.

Charney, Dennis S, and Southwick, Steven. 2018. *Resilience: The Science of Mastering Life's Greatest Challenges*. Cambridge, England: Cambridge University Press.

Cherry, Kendra. "Understanding the Psychology of Positive Thinking." *Verywell Mind*. November 26, 2019. Accessed September 18, 2020. https://www.verywellmind.com/what-is-positive-thinking-2794772.

Cherry, Kendra. 2019. "How Listening to Music Can Have Psychological Benefits." *Verywell Mind*. December 10, 2019. https://www.verywellmind.com/surprising-psychological-benefits-of-music-4126866.

Christakis, Nicholas and Fowler, James. 2008. "Social Networks and Happiness." Edge, December 4, 2008. http://www.edge.org/conversation/social-networks-and-happiness.

Cirillo, Francesco. 2020. The Pomodoro Technique. Accessed September 18, 2020. www.pomodorotechnique.com.

Clear, James. 2018. *Atomic Habits: An Easy & Proven Way to Build Good Habits & Break Bad Ones*. New York: Avery.

Contie, Vicki. 2007. "Brain Imaging Reveals Joys of Giving." *National Institutes of Health* (NIH), June 22, 2007. Accessed September 18, 2020. https://www.nih.gov/news-events/nih-research-matters/brain-imaging-reveals-joys-giving.

REFERENCES

Corley, Tom. 2016. *Change Your Habits, Change Your Life: Strategies that Transformed 177 Average People into Self-Made Millionaires.* Minneapolis, MN: North Loop Books.

Covey, Stephen. 2020. *The 7 Habits of Highly Effective People: 30th Anniversary Edition.* New York: Simon & Schuster.

Davies, Thomas. 2016. "How To Design Your Time." *Medium,* April 11, 2016. Accessed September 18, 2020. https://medium.com/gsuite/how-to-design-your-time-cf1a97a0d050.

Doran, George T. 1981. "There's a S.M.A.R.T. Way to Write Management's Goals and Objectives." *Management Review,* November.

Drucker, Peter F. 2006. *The Effective Executive: The Definitive Guide to Getting the Right Things Done.* New York: Harper Business.

Duhigg, Charles. 2014. *The Power of Habit: Why We Do What We Do in Life and Business.* New York: Random House.

Dweck, Carol S. 2007. *Mindset: The New Psychology of Success.* New York: Ballantine Books.

Emmons, Robert A. 2008 "Gratitude, Subjective Well-Being, and the Brain." *The Science of Subjective Well-Being* (p. 469–489), Larsen R. J., and Eid, M (Eds.). New York, NY: Guilford Press.

Emmons, Robert A, and McCullough, Michael E. 2003. "Counting Blessings versus Burdens: An Experimental Investigation of Gratitude and Subjective Well-Being in Daily Life." *Journal of Personality and Social Psychology,* 84, no. 2: 377–389. https://psycnet.apa.org/record/2003-01140-012.

Emmons, Robert and McCullough, Michael. 2004. *The Psychology of Gratitude.* New York, NY: Oxford University Press.

Emmons, Robert A, and McNamara, Patrick. 2006. "Sacred Emotions and Affective Neuroscience: Gratitude, Costly Signaling, and the Brain." in *Where God and Man Meet: How the Brain and Evolutionary Sciences are Revolutionizing Our Understanding of Religion and Spirituality* (p. 11–30), McNamara, Patrick (Ed). Westport, CT: Praeger Publishers.

Gielan, Michelle, and Achor, Shawn. 2017. "The Science of Changing Other People: Positive Psychology Guides the Way to a Happiness Ripple Effect." *Success,* August, 2017. https://www.questia.com/magazine/1G1-499719630/the-science-of-changing-other-people-positive-psychology and https://www.success.com/the-science-of-changing-other-people/.

Gillett, Rachel. 2015. "How Walt Disney, Oprah Winfrey, and 19 Other Successful People Rebounded After Getting Fired." *Inc.,* October, 2015.

https://www.inc.com/business-insider/21-successful-people-who-rebounded-after-getting-fired.html.

Glazer, Robert. 2019. "When People Ask How You Are, Stop Saying Busy." *Inc.*, February 11, 2019. Accessed September 18, 2020. https://www.inc.com/robert-glazer/when-people-ask-how-you-are-stop-saying-busy.html.

Grant, Adam. 2014. *Give and Take: A Revolutionary Approach to Success*. New York: Penguin Books.

Grimm Jr., Robert, Spring, Kimberly, and Dietz, Nathan. 2007. "The Health Benefits of Volunteering: A Review of Recent Research." Corporation for National and Community Service, Office of Research and Policy Development. Washington, DC. Accessed September 18, 2020. https://www.nationalservice.gov/pdf/07_0506_hbr.pdf.

Groppel, Jack. 2020. "Jack Groppel, Ph.D. Co-Founder of the Johnson & Johnson Human Performance Institute." Johnson & Johnson. Accessed September 18, 2020. https://www.jnj.com/jjhws/jack-groppel.

Harary, Charlie. 2018. *Unlocking Greatness: The Unexpected Journey From The Life You Have To The Life You Want*. Emmaus, PA: Rodale.

Hewlett, Sylvia Ann, and Luce, Carolyn Buck. 2006. "Extreme Jobs: The Dangerous Allure of the 70-Hour Workweek." *Harvard Business Review*, December 2006. Accessed September 18, 2020. https://hbr.org/2006/12/extreme-jobs-the-dangerous-allure-of-the-70-hour-workweek.

Holt-Lunstad, Julianne, Robles, Theodore F, and Sbarra, David A. 2017. "Advancing Social Connection as a Public Health Priority in the United States," *American Psychologist*, 72, no. 6: 517–530. https://www.apa.org/pubs/journals/releases/amp-amp0000103.pdf.

Holt-Lunstad, Julianne, Smith, Timothy B, Layton, J Bradley. 2010. "Social Relationships and Mortality Risk: A Meta-Analytic Review." *PLoS Medicine*, 7, no.7. https://pubmed.ncbi.nlm.nih.gov/20668659/.

Hyatt, Michael. 2020. *Full Focus Planner*. Accessed September 18, 2020. www.fullfocusplanner.com.

International Churchill Society. 2012. "Keep Calm and Carry On, The Real Story." Churchill Bulletin #45. Accessed September 18, 2020. https://winstonchurchill.org/publications/churchill-bulletin/bulletin-045-mar-2012/keep-calm-and-carry-on-the-real-story-1/.

Johns Hopkins Medical. 2020. "For Your Heart: Stay Calm and Cool." Accessed September 18, 2020. https://www.hopkinsmedicine.org/health/wellness-and-prevention/for-your-heart-stay-calm-and-cool.

REFERENCES

Killingsworth, Matthew A, and Gilbert, Daniel T. 2010. "A Wandering Mind Is an Unhappy Mind." *Science Mag*, November 11, 2010. Accessed September 18, 2020. http://wjh-www.harvard.edu/~dtg/KILLINGSWORTH%20&%20GILBERT%20%282010%29.pdf.

Life is Good. 2020. Accessed September 18, 2020. https://www.lifeisgood.com/.

Lin-Siegler, Xiadong, and Ahn, Janet N. 2016. "Even Einstein Struggled: Effects of Learning About Great Scientists' Struggles on High School Students' Motivation to Learn Science." Journal of Educational Psychology, 108, no. 3 (February 12): 314–328. https://www.apa.org/pubs/journals/releases/edu-edu0000092.pdf.

Lyubomirsky, Sonja. 2008. *The How of Happiness: A New Approach to Getting the Life You Want*. New York: Penguin Books.

Lyubomirsky, Sonja. 2020. "Sonja Lyubomirsky." Accessed September 18, 2020. http://sonjalyubomirsky.com/.

MacKay, Jory. 2019. "The State of Work Life Balance in 2019: What We Learned from Studying 185 Million Hours of Working Time." RescueTime, January 24, 2019. Accessed September 18, 2020. https://blog.rescuetime.com/work-life-balance-study-2019/.

MacKay, Jory. 2019. "Time Management Tips & Strategies: 25 ways to be more efficient at work," RescueTime, September 10, 2019. Accessed September 18, 2020. https://blog.rescuetime.com/time-management/.

MacMillan, Amanda. 2017. "Being Generous Really Does Make You Happier." *Time*, July 14, 2017. Accessed September 18, 2020. https://time.com/4857777/generosity-happiness-brain/.

Marsh, Jason and Suttie, Jill. 2010. "5 Ways Giving Is Good for You." *Greater Good Magazine*, December 13, 2010. Accessed September 18, 2020. https://greatergood.berkeley.edu/article/item/5_ways_giving_is_good_for_you.

Maslow, Abraham. 1954. *Motivation and Personality*. New York: Harper.

Meerson, Shirley. 2018. "6 Benefits of Being Calm." *Thrive Global*, July 16, 2018. Accessed September 18, 2020. https://thriveglobal.com/stories/6-benefits-of-being-calm-3/.

Montañez, Rachel. 2020. "This Work-Life Balance Study Reveals 3 Major Problems: Here's What We Need To Ask." *Forbes*, February 10, 2020. Accessed September 18, 2020. https://www.forbes.com/sites/rachelmontanez/2020/02/10/this-work-life-balance-study-reveals-3-major-problems-heres-what-we-need-to-ask/#18fdfc2a7277.

MORE

Moore, Catherine. 2020. "How to Set and Achieve Life Goals The Right Way." *Positive Psychology*, January 9, 2020. Accessed September 18, 2020. https://positivepsychology.com/life-worth-living-setting-life-goals/.

Morin, Amy. 2015. "13 Things Mentally Strong People Don't Do." *Psychology Today*, January 12, 2015. Accessed September 18, 2020. https://www.psychologytoday.com/us/blog/what-mentally-strong-people-dont-do/201501/13-things-mentally-strong-people-dont-do.

Morin, Amy. 2017. *13 Things Mentally Strong People Don't Do: Take Back Your Power, Embrace Change, Face Your Fears, and Train Your Brain for Happiness and Success*. New York: William Morrow.

Park, Soyoung Q, Kahnt, Thorsten, Dogan, Azade, Strang, Sabrina, Fehr, Ernst, and Tobler, Philippe N. 2017. "A Neural Link Between Generosity and Happiness." *Nature Communications*, July 11, 2017. Accessed September 18, 2020. https://www.nature.com/articles/ncomms15964.

Parker-Pope, Tara. 2017. "How to Build Resilience in Midlife." *The New York Times*, July 25, 2017. https://www.nytimes.com/2017/07/25/well/mind/how-to-boost-resilience-in-midlife.html.

Pausch, Randy, and Zaslow, Jeffrey. 2008. *The Last Lecture*. Westport, CT: Hyperion.

Peace Love World. 2020. Accessed September 18, 2020. https://www.peaceloveworld.com/.

Perlow, Leslie and Porter, Jessica. 2009. "Making Time Off Predictable-and Required." *Harvard Business Review*, October 2009. https://hbr.org/2009/10/making-time-off-predictable-and-required.

Pew Research Center. 2019. "Social Media Fact Sheet." June 12, 2019. Accessed September 18, 2020. https://www.pewresearch.org/internet/fact-sheet/social-media/.

Pink, Daniel H. 2018. *The Scientific Secrets of Perfect Timing*. New York: Riverhead Books.

Prichard, Skip. 2018. *The Book of Mistakes: 9 Secrets to Creating a Successful Future*. New York: Center Street.

Raim, Ianna. www.iannaraimcoaching.com Career and Leadership Consulting and Coaching.

Richards, Suzanne. 2013. "Go On, Volunteer – It Could Be Good for You!" University of Exeter, August 23, 2013. Accessed September 18, 2020. https://www.exeter.ac.uk/news/featurednews/title_315358_en.html.

REFERENCES

Robbins, Tony. 2018. "Tony Robbins' Ultimate Guide to Your Best Year Ever." *Success Magazine,* December 3, 2018. Accessed September 18, 2020. https://www.tonyrobbins.com/news/how-to-have-your-best-year-yet/.

Rohrer, Julia M, Richter, David, Brummer, Martin, Wagner, Gert G, and Schmukle, Stefan C. 2018. "Successfully Striving for Happiness: Socially Engaged Pursuits Predict Increases In Life Satisfaction." *Psychological Science,* 29, no.8. https://journals.sagepub.com/doi/abs/10.1177/0956797618761660.

Rubin, Gretchin. 2012. "Carl Jung's Five Key Elements to Happiness." *Psychology Today,* Accessed September 18, 2020. https://www.psychologytoday.com/au/blog/the-happiness-project/201202/carl-jungs-five-key-elements-happiness.

Sachs, Israel Joe. 2010. *Legacy of Life: A Memoir of the Holocaust.* Wisconsin: MavenMark Books.

Sandberg, Sheryl and Grant, Adam. 2017. *Option B: Facing Adversity, Building Resilience, and Finding Joy.* New York: Knopf.

Santi, Jenni. 2016. *The Giving Way to Happiness: Stories and Science Behind the Life-Changing Power of Giving.* New York: Tarcher-Perigee.

Santi, Jenny. 2017. "The Secret to Happiness Is Helping Others." *Time,* August 4, 2017. Accessed September 18, 2020. https://time.com/4070299/secret-to-happiness/.

Santi, Jenny. 2015. "The Science Behind the Power of Giving" *Live Science,* December 01, 2015 Accessed September 18, 2020. https://www.livescience.com/52936-need-to-give-boosted-by-brain-science-and-evolution.html.

Santos, Laurie. 2020. "Department of Psychology: People – Laurie Santos." Accessed September 18, 2020. https://psychology.yale.edu/people/laurie-santos.

Santos, Laurie. 2020. "The Science of Well-Being." Accessed September 18, 2020. https://www.coursera.org/learn/the-science-of-well-being.

Segal, Amy Klein. Spinning instructor. @spinmoma on Instagram. @amykleinsegal on Facebook.

Seligman, Martin E.P. 2004. *Authentic Happiness: Using the New Positive Psychology to Realize Your Potential for Lasting Fulfillment.* New York: Atria Book.

Shakya, Holly B, and Christakis, Nicholas A. 2017. "Association of Facebook Use With Compromised Well-Being: A Longitudinal Study," *American Journal of Epidemiology,* 185, no. 3 (February 1, 2017): 203–211. https://academic.oup.com/aje/article/185/3/203/2915143.

MORE

Silverstein, Shel. 1964. *The Giving Tree*. New York: Harper & Row.

Simmons, Michael. 2020. "Michael Simmons: About." Accessed September 18, 2020. http://michaeldsimmons.com/bio/.

Su, Elizabeth. 2018. "What Gratitude Does To Your Brain." Thrive Global, November 27, 2018. https://thriveglobal.com/stories/gratitude-brain-positive-change-thank-you/.

Sull, Donald, and Sull, Charles. 2018. "With Goals, FAST Beats SMART." MIT Sloan Management Review, June 05, 2018. Accessed September 18, 2020. https://sloanreview.mit.edu/article/with-goals-fast-beats-smart/.

Turkle, Sherry. 2012. "Connected, But Alone." TEDtalk. Accessed September 18, 2020. https://www.ted.com/talks/sherry_turkle_connected_but_alone.

Vanderkam, Laura. 2011. *168 Hours: You Have More Time Than You Think*. London: Portfolio.

Vaillant, Dr. George . 2003. *Aging Well: Surprising Guideposts to a Happier Life from the Landmark Harvard Study of Adult Development*. New York: Little, Brown Spark.

World Happiness Report. 2020. "World Happiness Report." Accessed September 18, 2020. https://worldhappiness.report/.

Yanek, Lisa R, Kral, Brian G, Moy, Taryn F, Vaidya, Dhananjay, Lazo, Mariana, Becker, Lewis C, and Becker, Diane M. 2013. "Effect of Positive Well-Being on Incidence of Symptomatic Coronary Artery Disease." *American Journal of Cardiology*, 112, no. 8 (October 15): 1120–1125. https://www.ajconline.org/article/S0002-9149(13)01280-0/fulltext.

Young, Susan. 2020. "Yale Student Who Grew Up Homeless Reveals How She Achieved Goals: 'Keep Your Eyes on the Prize'." *People*, May 28, 2020. Accessed September 18, 2020. https://people.com/human-interest/yale-student-who-grew-up-homeless-reveals-how-she-achieved-goals/.

Zahn, Roland, Garrido, Griselda, Moll, Jorge, and Grafman, Jordan. 2014. "Individual Differences in Posterior Cortical Volume Correlate with Proneness to Pride and Gratitude." *Social Cognitive and Affective Neuroscience*. 9, no. 11 (November): 1676–1683. https://www.ncbi.nlm.nih.gov/pmc/articles/PMC4221203/.

Zahn, Roland, Moll, Jorge, Paiva, Mirella, Garrido, Griselda, Krueger, Frank, Huey, Edward, and Grafman, Jordan. 2008. "The Neural Basis of Human Social Values: Evidence from Functional MRI." *Cerebral Cortex*, 19, no. 2 (February): 276–283. https://www.ncbi.nlm.nih.gov/pmc/articles/PMC2733324/.

Acknowledgements

Many of the life lessons and anecdotes described in this book have been inspired by incredible people I have encountered throughout my life. I am blessed to be supported by a loving and strong support system. What I have realized in recent years is how important every experience, both good and bad, has been in shaping my life. I believe every person serves a different purpose in your life. There are numerous people I want to acknowledge in helping me get to this point.

Thank you Natasa and Stuart Denman, Vivienne Mason, Marinda Wilkinson, and Amy Ryan for helping me through this writing and editing process. Your expertise, patience and guidance were vital to the completion of this book. I want to thank Tammy, Rochelle, Mimi, Matt, Lili, Jeannette, Ann, and Tara for your invaluable advice regarding this manuscript and your friendship. Shout out to Ana for your inspirational words that led to the title. I have so much gratitude for Amy G. for her photography and support.

Thanks to my forever friends from NMB, Beth, Eve, Mindy, Pam, Sheryl, and Jami for teaching me that there is such a thing as unconditional and long-lasting friendship. Special shout out to Sheryl for offering to do the foreword to this book. Thanks to my Columbia friends for over 30 years of friendship. Thanks to every friend who shared Camp Elise with me by contributing to one of the best weekends of my life and becoming a catalyst to pursuing this project. Each of your friendships has added something special to my life. I appreciate the groups I have been a part of that have brought me wisdom, joy, and support—my book club, Colorado girls, Amenta sisters, Dimess, Poland ladies, NWP, WP, Legal ladies, Mastermind groups and the many organizations that I have been fortunate to be a part of in recent years. A special shout out to the many nonprofit leaders I have had the opportunity to work with to advance the betterment of our community. These unsung heroes, in my opinion, work tirelessly and effectively to help others and improve this world.

To my family, I am blessed to be surrounded by aunts, uncles, and cousins who are loving, caring and fun. The Roks, Schecks, Berezdivins, Morjains, and Moskovitz and their families have had an indelible mark on my life and I treasure the times that we are together. To Tia Rosita, Ely, and Evelyn, thank you for "getting me" and sharing it all. Not sure where I would be without the love, camaraderie, and support of my siblings, Adrienne and Jeffrey Scheck, Hili and Marty Scheck and Michele and Steven Scheck and my nieces and nephews, Zachary, Carli, Faryn, Nikki, Dani, Shelby, Amanda, Jenna, Evan, Alexa, Haley, and Adam. I am grateful that we share everything and anything—and I would not have it any other way. I adore and appreciate each of you.

To my parents, Raquel and Michael Scheck—who have been incredible role models to me. I can never thank you enough for your love, inspiration, and wisdom. To my husband Gil

ACKNOWLEDGEMENTS

Bonwitt—the best and most important decision I have ever made. Thank you for your love, respect and encouragement. I would not be able to do any of this without you. At times, you have believed in me more than I believed in myself and I feel blessed to share this life with you. To my children, Joshua, Keith, David, Gabriella, and Jessica—words cannot adequately express the pride, joy, gratitude, and love I feel for each of you. I could literally write a book on each of you and describe how you bring MORE of everything into my life.

About the Author

Elise is an attorney, mediator, business owner, consultant, and coach. Currently a principal at Scheck Group, a family office, she is also a Certified Circuit Court Mediator, mediating cases across areas of corporate litigation, employment law, real estate, probate, insurance, and personal injury.

As the co-founder of the website Amenta, (www. shopamenta.com) she supports artisans and their communities throughout Latin America to sell their products online. In addition, she is the co-founder of SImpact (www.simpact. it), an organization committed to increasing performance of social sector organizations.

Elise has been actively involved in several nonprofit organizations, and has given her time and energy to numerous boards and committees throughout Miami. She is a Partner with Social Venture Partners, a member of the National Women's Philanthropy Board, a board member of Overtown Youth Center and a Mentor with Women of Tomorrow, where she works with 30 girls at a local school. She is also involved with Greater Miami Jewish Federation and is currently a Vice

Chair of the Board. She was chair of the Women's Impact Initiative and President of Women's Philanthropy, among other leadership positions.

Elise graduated from University of Miami Law School and Columbia University and completed the Executive Program in Social Impact Strategy at the University of Pennsylvania. She enjoys spinning, running, reading, mahjong, and participating in volunteer opportunities with her children. She lives in Miami with her husband, Gil, and they are the proud parents of five children.

For more information or to get in touch,
visit www.getmorewithless.com